On King Lear, The Confessions, and Human Experience and Nature

READING AUGUSTINE

Series Editor:
Miles Hollingworth

Reading Augustine presents books that offer personal, nuanced and oftentimes literary readings of Saint Augustine of Hippo. Each time, the idea is to treat Augustine as a spiritual and intellectual icon of the Western tradition, and to read through him to some or other pressing concern of our current day. Or to some enduring issue or theme. In this way, the writers follow the model of Augustine himself, who produced his famous output of words and ideas in active tussle with the world in which he lived. When the series launched, this approach could raise eyebrows, but now that technology and pandemics have brought us into the world and society like never before, and when scholarship is expected to live the same way and responsibly, the series is well-set and thriving.

Volumes in the series:

On Music, Sense, Affect, and Voice, Carol Harrison
On Solitude, Conscience, Love and Our Inner, and Outer Lives, Ron Haflidson
On Creation, Science, Disenchantment, and the Contours of Being and Knowing, Matthew W. Knotts
On Agamben, Arendt, Christianity, and the Dark Arts of Civilization, Peter Iver Kaufman
On Self-Harm, Narcissism, Atonement, and the Vulnerable Christ, David Vincent Meconi
On Faith, Works, Eternity, and the Creatures We Are, André Barbera
On Time, Change, History, and Conversion, Sean Hannan
On Compassion, Healing, Suffering, and the Purpose of the Emotional Life, Susan Wessel
On Consumer Culture, Identity, the Church and the Rhetorics of Delight, Mark Clavier
On Creativity, Liberty, Love and the Beauty of the Law, Todd Breyfogle
On Education, Formation, Citizenship and the Lost Purpose of Learning, Joseph Clair
On Ethics, Politics and Psychology in the Twenty-First Century, John Rist
On God, The Soul, Evil and the Rise of Christianity, John Peter Kenney
On Love, Confession, Surrender and the Moral Self, Ian Clausen
On Memory, Marriage, Tears, and Meditation, Margaret R. Miles

On King Lear, The Confessions, and Human Experience and Nature

Kim Paffenroth

BLOOMSBURY ACADEMIC
LONDON • NEW YORK • OXFORD • NEW DELHI • SYDNEY

BLOOMSBURY ACADEMIC
Bloomsbury Publishing Inc
50 Bedford Square, London, WC1B 3DP, UK
1385 Broadway, New York, NY 10018, USA
29 Earlsfort Terrace, Dublin 2, Ireland

BLOOMSBURY, BLOOMSBURY ACADEMIC and the Diana logo
are trademarks of Bloomsbury Publishing Plc

First published in Great Britain 2021

A catalogue record for this book is available from the British Library.

Library of Congress Cataloging-in-Publication Data
Names: Paffenroth, Kim, 1966- author.
Title: On King Lear, The confessions, and human
experience and nature / Kim Paffenroth.
Description: New York : Bloomsbury Academic, 2022. |
Series: Reading Augustine | Includes bibliographical references and index. |
Identifiers: LCCN 2020045173 (print) | LCCN 2020045174 (ebook)
| ISBN 9781350203198 (paperback) | ISBN 9781350203204 (hardback)
| ISBN 9781350203211 (epub) | ISBN 9781350203228 (pdf)
Subjects: LCSH: Shakespeare, William, 1564-1616.
King Lear. | Augustine, of Hippo, Saint, 354-430. Confessiones.
Classification: LCC PR2819 .P29 2022 (print) | LCC PR2819 (ebook) |
DDC 822.3/3–dc23
LC record available at https://lccn.loc.gov/2020045173
LC ebook record available at https://lccn.loc.gov/2020045174

ISBN: HB: 978-1-3502-0320-4
PB: 978-1-3502-0319-8
ePDF: 978-1-3502-0322-8
ePUB: 978-1-3502-0321-1

Typeset by Integra Software Services Pvt. Ltd.
Printed and bound in Great Britain

To find out more about our authors and books visit www.bloomsbury.com
and sign up for our newsletters.

CONTENTS

ACKNOWLEDGMENTS

I have to acknowledge first the persistence, enthusiasm, and insight of the *Reading Augustine* series editor, Miles Hollingworth. Repeatedly over the last couple years he asked me to write a book for his series. I am at a point in my career where administrative tasks seemed overwhelming and I thought would never allow such a writing project. But Miles kept asking. And then in the midst of the disorienting, demoralizing adversity of the pandemic, as much as it might seem I had plenty of time, it definitely did not seem to me I had the strength or focus for such work. But still he asked, and it finally sounded to me like Monica eventually sounded to Augustine—the providential voice, speaking for his/her own reasons, but moving me to a purpose God intended: "Our good abides ever in your keeping" (*Conf.* 4.16.31).[1] Miles's perseverance paid off, and was followed by many more communications of encouragement and support. He has been an exemplary scholar and collaborator, though we have never met in person.

As my Introduction will try to explain, I find it very difficult to know how far back to take acknowledgments, without following Augustine's lead and going back to the womb (and it is true that, born premature and way underweight, I very likely wouldn't be here to write this, were it not for many obstetrics doctors and nurses, all those years ago, so I see Augustine's point, if for very different reasons than he expressed, and I have many times thought of those people, and more so this year, during a plague, as everyone's attention is directed to medical personnel). But for a less expansive sense of acknowledging those who played a more direct part in this current work, I would at least have to go back to St. John's College, where I first read the books we'll be considering here. I have often thought that for a St. John's graduate, laboring in academia outside of "the college" (as it is referred to by all in the community, the way true believers in any denomination refer to "the Church" without any further specification), there is always a huge advantage in writing and expressing oneself about the texts we examine, from our time at St. John's and the habits we learned there. While at St. John's we are constantly pushed to consider what the books are about, rather than ask questions about the books or authors (or movements or epochs or audiences or all the myriad things that distract our colleagues and students elsewhere). That particular insight got hammered into me in my first semester there, at a particularly humbling first paper conference (and all the conferences on my many inept, inarticulate papers there were humbling, when they were not outright humiliating), by my freshmen seminar tutors (professors at St. John's are called "tutors" and eschew the title "Dr."), Ms. Patricia Locke and Mr. John White. I always think of everything I've ever written since my time there, as an attempt to redeem myself by writing better than I did while there, but in the same spirit and with the same purpose: to analyze texts and synthesize ideas into something clear and insightful, to do something playful and yet meaningful with the ideas we encounter—goals St. John's filled me with a passion to achieve, but only many years of practice and struggle since have slightly better equipped me to actually accomplish. So I should single out for thanks, Br. Robert Smith and Mr. David Townsend, the St. John's tutors with whom I first read *Confessions*, and Mr. Joe Sachs, also of St. John's, with whom I first read *King Lear*. For more recent and ongoing interactions and support, I think Mr. John Verdi of St. John's has most frequently and consistently put up with the ramblings of my mediocre mind over the many years since we met, encouraging me in my writing, teaching, and now in my work as an administrator.

I would also like to thank the staff at Iona College's Ryan Library, under the direction of Richard Palladino. I note especially Ed Helmrich and his staff in the Interlibrary Loan office, for their help in obtaining books and articles from other libraries, and Natalka Sawchuk, Assistant Director of Libraries, for help getting books out of the Iona library when it was closed during the pandemic.

Robert P. Kennedy again performed proofreading duties, as he has on many previous works of mine, and again must be thanked for this loyal service. I also thank Nicole Genser, one of my most gifted and hardest working students at Iona, for helping with the final proofreading of the manuscript.

If this book began with my teachers, it has grown and now come together with my students, in all the happy and demanding hours we have spent thinking and talking together. I have dedicated books before to my students; I have mentioned them, sometimes en masse, sometimes naming specific ones, in almost every book I've ever written. They have been my companions on so many voyages, my coworkers on so many projects—intellectual ones through these and other texts, but in the last several years, also working together more generally, as I have delegated more and more responsibilities to the students, for running the Iona College Honors Program. In both their academic work and their service to the Iona community, they have demonstrated they already knew to "speak what we feel, not what we ought to say" (*King Lear*, 5.3.384), and I have often looked upon them as Augustine looked upon Alypius: "I for my part was fond of him on account of his great nobility of character, which was unmistakable even before he reached mature years" (*Conf.* 6.7.11). They are also some of the ones who can best answer for me, the question Lear asks, "Who is it that can tell me who I am?" (*King Lear* 1.4.236). I have always known my only role as their teacher or director was to improve the elegance, clarity, and persuasiveness with which they expressed themselves, not to teach them either wisdom or virtue, which they constantly embody better than I do. I am blessed beyond words for having had the chance to get to know so many bright, young, gifted people, and to have benefited from their hard work, dedication, and generosity. A book so heavily dependent on my life and thought as a teacher has to be dedicated to them, and given the timing of this one, I will here specify the dedication to all those in the Iona College Honors Program, Class of 2020.

Note

1 Augustine, *The Confessions* (The Works of Saint Augustine: A Translation for the 21st Century, translated by Maria Boulding (Hyde Park, NY: New City Press, 2001). All quotations from *Confessions* are from this translation unless otherwise noted.

Introduction: The Problem of Time

For years I have offered theological readings or interpretations of great literature, or artifacts of popular culture. My process has always been to take a topic or concept, and find illustrations and elaborations within texts, and/or use the texts as contrasting views of a subject. And this current work will resemble my earlier approach in its devotion to close reading and immersion in the texts. But where I have finally seen a new approach here is to focus on just two texts, Augustine's *Confessions* and Shakespeare's *King Lear*, rather than the more diverse, broader groups of witnesses I have marshalled in previous works. What I want to do here is to take two texts that have spoken to me powerfully for thirty-five years, and pair them (yoke them, if I were being more forceful and violent, as I feel Lear or Augustine themselves had a tendency to be), to reveal together truths that each singly can reveal only partly. I suppose it will be deemed quaint in our postmodern world, but I may as well get such ideas out in the open at the beginning of this work: it almost seems to me that the texts had been intimating to me, inchoately but insistently, that such truths could be discovered by sensitive readers, who returned to these very different and difficult texts, over and over, and let them speak, to one another and to the reader (and the reader to them), out of love, sympathy, curiosity, and a devotion to the truth, shared across the centuries.[1]

So much for now, for the "what" of this book. (We'll return to details of that at the end of this Introduction.) Now as I begin this exploration with you, I am contemplating how it is, that considering an idea, its importance and meaning and nuances, immediately takes us into a consideration of time. Perhaps that is why Augustine includes a discussion on memory (Book X) and time (Book XI) in his *Confessions*—with the latter especially being a discussion notoriously more evocative than explanatory of anything—after he has discussed his life, the ideas and beliefs that have guided it (and been formed by it), what those ideas meant to him (in the past), what they mean to him at the time of writing, what access they might give him, or us, to eternal truths, or how they might make possible a relationship with an infinite, immortal God. Even without the discussion of time itself, the way he narrates and theorizes about his life shows that it is not just our existence or being that is problematic for us, but that our problematic nature is only compounded by thinking about and sharing stories of our existence. And yet, and much more poignantly, remaining silent, saying, "Nothing," as in the other text we'll be examining together, Shakespeare's *King Lear*, is not a solution or even an option, because mere immediacy and immersion in experience, as pleasant and invigorating as it often is, is finally no solution, brings no lasting satisfaction, either. We humans are many things, and we are too often careless and oblivious, but I believe all but the most lost and debased persons are finally and completely creatures that examine and draw connections among the things to which we devote our attention. That drive to know and explain has to be followed, but it finally comes up as frustrated and frustrating, the more it has discovered, because the remaining realm of the unknown taunts and mocks it, not only refusing to surrender, but not even retreating, as ever more unknowns are discovered (but still not understood). I think this is what the teacher/poet has in mind in one of the most tantalizing and revealing lines of the Bible, when he writes how God "has put a sense of past and future into their minds, yet they cannot find out what God has done from the beginning to the end" (Eccl. 3:11 [NRSV]). We are built, hard-wired (or, since Darwin, evolved), to be restless seekers of truth, always on the move, and exactly as Augustine describes himself and us at the beginning of his *Confessions*: "Our heart is unquiet until it rests in you" (*Conf.* 1.1.1).

So to recollect a specific example of this problem for myself, unrelated to the current project: when I felt the need (and saw the popularity) of explaining why zombies mean something to me and many others, I had to first think to myself, "Why? How?" And I had answers to those questions, but they took me quickly to a question of time I had not anticipated, "When?" This might seem trivial or simple at first, but I think it turns out to be the more difficult of those questions. What is the crucial point in time for an idea? When it begins? Or when it reaches whatever conclusion it is meant to? (Or if we want to exclude something so teleological—the conclusion it just happens to reach, historically?) Or more modestly, even, where should I start the examination of this particular idea? The first time I saw a zombie movie? The second time, which was the first in a theater, and is the experience I recollect more vividly? The time more recently, when all the memories came flooding back, because I'd just seen a zombie film for the first time in twenty years, and I had many more ideas and experiences to which to relate it, much more theory and language with which to analyze it? And whichever part of the timeline I pick, how do I include consideration of how zombies might have meant something very different to me when I was thirteen than when I was thirty-eight (or now, when I'm fifty-five)? And if different, how are those various meanings related? Is there (God forbid) a hierarchy? Or why am I even thinking of myself and my timeline? Why not claim (or at least strive for) objectivity, and go back to the first zombie film ever made? Or the first zombie story? Or the first zombie myth? Or, if zombies are related to other kinds of undead, why not back to all the films, stories, and myths of vampires, ghouls, and ghosts? What seemed like a very specific, circumscribed question turned into something very disparate and elusive, as well as exciting and broad and interconnected, indeed.

Years later, and on topics no less important than zombies, I find myself similarly befuddled as to time, and I can only begin by begging some indulgence, and some allowance for flexibility in how I present the ideas herein. Each chapter will probably find us considering anecdotes or experiences or interpretations that occurred anywhere over thirty-five years of reading, studying, thinking over, and teaching these texts. But while a discussion can be free-wheeling and less linear than we are typically used to, it seems an introduction especially has to start *somewhere*. Words and communication in general are time specific by their very nature, shaped by time, only having meaning if they come at us in the right order, not as a swarm or fog, as Augustine notes in his discussion of time (*Conf.* 11.6.8; 11.28.38). And so here I was, all set to start by telling you when I first read these two texts—that should surely be far enough back, to treat it as a starting point. But no, then I realized

Augustine had it right: you have to go even further back, not just to the beginning of the hearing or reading, but to the beginning of the hearer or reader.

I will spare you infancy, though we will get to Augustine's theorizing on that soon enough. But *how* I came to read these texts bears some consideration. Like Augustine, I remember my parents as mostly well-meaning but profoundly unhappy with one another, and with their lives in general, for reasons I could not comprehend as a child, and which are now irretrievably and forever lost, years after their deaths. Also like Monica and Patricius, they were proud of me and poured a lot of their hopes and ambitions on to me. (And unlike Augustine, who one might assume, from a cursory reading of *Confessions*, had no siblings, I really was an only child, and did not have to share their parental attention, or fight others for it, like the supposedly jealous baby Augustine describes at *Conf.* 1.7.11). My father had been the first in his family to graduate college—eight years of night school at the Newark College of Engineering (since given the much more august title, The New Jersey Institute of Technology), while working full-time during the day. And I remember how he was never really proud of that accomplishment, as he never considered it "real" college. And I remember how, in those pre-internet days, he faithfully kept an article—I think from the *New Yorker* but it might have been another magazine—carefully clipped and preserved between plastic sheets and then stuck in a manila folder, that described the education at St. John's College. My father was never sentimental, nostalgic, or prone to hoarding things: there were few objects left to remember my mother when she died in 1980, and even fewer when he died in 2004. I know my entire time growing up, I had seen few objects or even photos that predated my birth, and my parents had moved numerous times before I was born, and several more times during my childhood. My father didn't have a fear of materialism or ostentation, really—he enjoyed pleasures and possessions (which may come up in this analysis). But he had a horror of accumulating attachments, or even reminders of attachments, that I can barely imagine. He lived his entire life never owning a home. Throughout his life (at least after 1980), right up until the end, he bragged that he could throw most of all his possessions in the back seat of his car, and move on to another adventure, at a moment's notice. I remember when I told him I'd bought a home, and then when

I'd gotten tenure: both times he could not express congratulations or happiness, because what I'd done was incomprehensible to him, nearly abhorrent, if not an outright repudiation of his lifestyle and choices, so he could only complain, "Why'd you do that? Now it'll be harder for you to leave." He would have been less confused or alarmed, if I'd told him I'd joined a cult—because in a way, from his perspective, I had. If Augustine and I characterize the human condition as one of restless seeking, always on the move, my father vividly and consistently embodied the restless and moving parts of that description; whether there was seeking involved, or for what, will now have to remain a mystery.

I give this brief and very partial (and yes, biased) biography of my father now, only to show that carefully preserving and carrying around a magazine article for twenty or thirty years (I don't know if the original article predated my existence but it definitely predated my college search by many years) was hardly typical of him, when he carelessly allowed many more objects to drift in and out of his possession, in and out of existence. So that act of preservation bears a bit more scrutiny. I stand by my analysis that he abhorred attachments or mementoes, but these couple sheets of paper were not that. He had no real connection to St. John's College: he carried around a little talisman of the *idea* of St. John's, of this thing he'd never partaken of, personally. Lest one think I'm just advertising for my alma mater (or worse, bragging about it), let's say my father idolized the idea of a liberal arts education, of an education that maintained and enshrined the idea that knowledge is emphatically *not* instrumental, but a good in itself. If St. John's did or does a good job of communicating that value or belief, then they have done a good job of "branding" and other liberal arts colleges may wish to take note as they struggle to strengthen their "brand" and survive in the current market (which was already difficult enough, even before our current plague). But it was the idea of a higher purpose and existence than mere utilitarian concerns that fascinated and enthralled him, and to which level he felt his own education never rose.

I myself remember the article as equal parts admiration and bemusement, the way one would describe the dedication with which medieval monks copied manuscripts, or groupies followed their favorite band back and forth across the continent—lifestyles at some extreme remove from the sickened, materialistic, selfish modern world, and therefore refreshing and a little admirable, but also just plain funny, weird, and obsessive in their own right. But whatever and however the article described it, it held only slightly less fascination for me than for my father, probably compounded by being surrounded during high school by the children of physicists, chemists, and engineers who were quite focused on a narrowly scientific education and career, and my own intense desire to stand out in some way from the herd. Throw in a high school history teacher who had gotten her master's at St. John's and was nearly as vocal and zealous as my father in praising the school and "The Program" (our name for St. John's set program of study, focused on and emanating from the Great Books). You might as well add that I was only a couple years away from having lost my mother, and therefore the idea that education or life has a higher purpose, and we're not just here to make money, pay taxes, and then die suddenly (or slowly), would find an especially enthusiastic believer in me. All these disparate and totally unplanned (and in the case of my mother's death, wholly unwelcome) factors came together and I was sold on the ideas of seminars, close reading of texts, a community of learners, a life of the mind, and considering ideas for their own sake and not whether they could be turned into a profit-making venture, or to improve one's material well-being, because ideas were meant to improve one's immaterial (and more important and fundamental) well-being.

That was how I came to first encounter these texts, a few months apart, in 1985 and 1986, strongly convinced (though very vague on the details or possible outcomes) that they must be important, contain important truths and insights that related to living, but not to making a living. Of course, part of St. John's, or of a liberal arts education more broadly, is that all great texts and ideas should be treated that way and encountered with that openness, respect, and trust, read as though they have something still (and always) relevant to say, and not just artifacts of a bygone age, replaced by new and better truths of ours. So did *Confessions* and *King Lear* stand out from the rest of the works I read at that time? Did I offer special insights into them, during class discussions? Did I write my senior essay on either? Was I inspired or uplifted by specific points of interpretation, given by brilliant teachers in class when discussing them? Given my above musings on time, it should be less of a surprise that I say "No" to all these interesting but contrafactual possibilities. That a lifelong fascination with these texts began thirty-five years ago and continued and grew and matured steadily until the present day, would be far too linear and logical and consistent, when part of the point of either text, or of my analysis of them here, is that three less appropriate adjectives could hardly be found to describe our lives than linear, logical, and consistent. At the time I was impressed and challenged by these two texts, as I was by many others I also read at that time, in a powerful but by no means unique way.

In some ways my thinking about these texts lay dormant for years during graduate school as I was studying the New Testament (another text I had only read for the first time in college). But I think I might have guessed throughout that time, that although I focused on something very narrow during graduate school (as one does, given how Ph.D. studies are conducted at present), I would always want to return to the more interdisciplinary thinking and learning that is (or should be) the hallmark of an undergraduate liberal arts education. I do recall that I never wanted to spend my life as "the expert" on any very narrow topic, and I regarded expertise as a waystation on a journey, or a rung on a ladder one was climbing, intellectually, to show depth before returning to consider the breadth of knowledge. I was "the expert" on the uniquely Lukan parables for a couple years, because I'd written a dissertation on them that became a book, with hundreds of footnotes, but all that meant to me was that that box had been checked off, that hurdle cleared. As I began teaching, I found it exciting and energizing to do with my students, what my undergraduate teachers had done with me, years before—help them see connections between texts, have them comparing and contrasting them, have them analyzing the developments and nuances of ideas.

So interdisciplinarity is perhaps easy enough to explain in my work, as it's been a lifelong commitment, but I still have to give you (and myself) at least a plausible reason for why I'm writing and you're reading about these two texts, specifically. Ultimately, it's the same answer as to the question, "Why did Augustine write *Confessions* (either as to its specific contents, or the general fact of having written such a book)?" Why? Because of his particular parents, siblings, child, friends, lovers, jobs he was offered or quit, books he read, people who spoke to him, writing contests he won, drunks he saw on the street, gladiators he saw die in the arena.[2] I think when we ask the question, we are too much looking for continuity (as I derided above), but also for some kind of essentialism, as though to answer the question of why someone wrote a particular book is tied up with who that person is, essentially or really, when it's more about the sum total of accidents that have made up his/her life. And really, we should also be open to those two extremes of explanation not being as far apart as we might like or imagine. That is what makes *Confessions* so perplexing and yet so sincere and authentic, because it is both a bunch of accidents (sometimes so much so they strain credulity) and a collection of them that, the author seems desperately trying to convince himself and us, are really providential, meaningful, and even blessed.

So through a series of accidents and choices, that seemed completely disconnected at the time, these two texts kept being pulled into my orbit, or I into theirs. Probably the biggest accident (or providential event) that determined much of my professional life is that my first full-time teaching job after graduate school was at Villanova University. (And that based on other unlikely coincidences—that Jack Doody, the man hiring me at Nova, was a graduate of Notre Dame; that John Cavadini, one of my teachers at Notre Dame, had previously taught and left a favorable impression at Nova.) It takes little imagination to think that if it had been somewhere else (as it surely could have been), I would not have been steered into a career so centered on Augustine (though my own limitations and interests always meant I was going to be a student of *Confessions*, and never anything as impressive-sounding as "an Augustine scholar," which I have never described myself as, anywhere, in public or private). *King Lear* has not been as central to my career and research, but it has been a recurring part of my teaching. Since 1993, I have repeatedly chosen to teach interdisciplinary freshmen seminars (see above on St. John's, for why that might keep recurring). They have been the most consistent part of my teaching throughout my career, and they usually involve coming up with a syllabus that is mixed as to genre, subject, and time period, so a Shakespeare play and an autobiography that could also pass as theology or philosophy were practical choices. I found the discussions these two texts elicited to be good, and to fit in with other texts, lead to other ideas, and become part of really excellent student writing—at Notre Dame, Villanova, and Iona College. Even so, I had been *Lear*-less for several years, until Iona College changed its core curriculum in 2017 and added a regular freshmen seminar (it had always had a freshmen seminar for Honors students), and I have again taught it there since, often simultaneous with teaching *Confessions* in the Honors seminar. And really, since I'm stressing the accidental and unpredictable and serendipitous at this point in my introduction and discussion, I think I will give more emphasis to that unplanned connection. I would never be teaching the two texts at the same time, unless I was simultaneously teaching two different seminars with different syllabuses. Every teacher has those moments, of thinking to explain one text by connecting it to another already examined in class, but in this case, that was constantly thwarted, because the regular seminar didn't read *Confessions*, and the Honors group didn't read *King Lear*. So I have had twenty-eight years of teaching these two texts in different settings, and four years now of teaching them simultaneously with each other, to see the kinds of connections I want to explore with you here. None of that happened with a plan to produce such thoughts or such a book, but here they are.

That is how I would try to tie together now, what I have been wondering about time and how it affects our encounters with truth. I am now considering time in the sense of our being utterly contingent on and limited by it. I will assume throughout this book that these two texts (and to be clear, many others) put us in touch with timeless, eternal truths. I could go further and say these texts put our eternal souls in contact with eternal goodness, truth, and beauty, and equip the soul itself to become better, more beautiful, and truer. But I remind myself constantly that I only came to believe that by a rather unlikely—I might almost say absurd—combination of temporal events that caused me to be a particular kind of reader, at a particular time, in a particular place, reading particular texts, surrounded by other particular people, each on their own unique journey that only very briefly intersected mine. But believe it I do, unlike many other things I believed thirty-five years ago, that the experiences of a temporal, contingent existence can nonetheless put one in touch with eternal and ultimate realities. That paradox of a contingent, mortal being, being brought into contact with and knowledge of the eternal and ultimate, precisely through and because of all its contingent, temporal experiences, is at the heart of *Confessions*—it is the paradoxical life Augustine struggles to describe to us. How much easier to describe a life of repudiating the earthly, of retreat from it, of ascetical or philosophical rejection of earthly ties[3]; how much easier in a different way, to describe a celebration and perfection of the earthly and heroic virtues. Both Augustine and I read texts that followed either of those other models, and we found much there to admire and inspire us. But he wrote and I read one that took it in that other direction, of paradox and humility, what one scholar has called "getting over oneself,"[4] but in a way that allows or demands one finally, authentically be oneself. Similarly, Shakespeare told many more conventionally satisfying stories of the fall of a great hero. What he tells us in *King Lear* of course follows much of the patterns of tragedy, but I believe the play finds its grandeur by it being finally a different kind of fall, of a different kind of hero, with a different kind of (possible) redemption, paradoxical in all its parts, and implying quite different things about what kind of creatures we are, or can be.

That finally is the truth of which these texts convinced me. Or put the other way around: that is the fundamental conviction of mine that they tapped into and gave me two of my deepest experiences of this belief in action. Whether they caused or resulted from the belief (or, more likely, both) is, like the question of time and ordering, probably indeterminable by our limited human faculties or investigation. That they have been part of my life and belief for most of my life, and all of my adult life, is finally all that I need to claim. And now, having more fully unpacked the "what" of this book, by way of discussing the "when," follow me now into the "how" of this exploration.

As I considered the idea of this book and of the *Reading Augustine* series, I went first to *King Lear*—because, as above, I've been teaching it to freshmen and having to explain its ideas, and hearing their reactions (made more difficult, and necessitating more thought on my part this past semester, by the sudden switch to online learning in reaction to the pandemic). And also because I wanted to test if the deep connections I sensed between the play and *Confessions* could be borne out by trying to map one text's concerns against the other. And I didn't want, in a series on Augustine, to give pride of place to the bishop of Hippo and let him first determine the parameters or ordering: better and more revealing of him, if his ancient thought can be subjected to a Shakespearean framework and analysis, than to give an Augustinian interpretation to Shakespeare. I think in a strange and beautiful way, the connections were better than I'd first hoped, and probably not in the ways I expected; equally exciting and challenging will be the ways these connections will change over the course of writing this book.

So considering the play and how I had discussed it with students over the years, I knew I had to start at the beginning, with Lear's mad and fatal query, "Which of you shall we say doth love us most?" (*King Lear* 1.1.56).[5] The play is surely first about very flawed ideas and expressions of love, and some very noble attempts at loving better.[6] Turning to *Confessions*, that is a good way to summarize much of Augustine's spiritual and intellectual journey—he is trying out different kinds of faulty love, on variously inappropriate objects of love. What is perhaps most similar between the two texts is how desperately *everyone needs* to love in both. Shakespeare has a thing for icy villains (e.g., Iago) but Goneril, Regan, and Cornwall have been the most explosive, out of control characters I've ever seen on stage; and Edmund, whom Bloom fits into the Iago mold of total negation and control,[7] can also be played with recklessness and passion. It's part of why it's so exhausting to see the play performed live. And I'm surely not giving anything away or prejudicing anyone when I say many readers would say the pear tree theft in Book Two of *Confessions* is one of the most overwrought things they've ever read. I would say more generally, these are two of the least Stoical or restrained texts I have experienced and taught, with everyone feeling and expressing everything—every slight, every desire, every impulse—constantly turned all the way up to eleven.[8] And the counsel from either text is not to be more restrained, but to be as outrageously devoted and passionate, but in the right way—a way perhaps even more difficult and demanding than the many, various wrong ways. That will begin our analysis here, for Chapter 1.

Staying in Act 1, scene 1 (and when I teach the play, we spend a disproportionate amount of our time on the first act, as there is so much there), I think we are forced by the daughters' responses, and even Lear's original request, to consider the problem of language. Though I think many times we paraphrase Lear as asking who loves him the most, his demand is just as much about language: "Which of you shall we *say* doth love us most?" (emphasis added), and repeated to each daughter, "Speak" (*King Lear* 1.1.59, 75, 95), culminating in a promise of reward to Cordelia, "what can you *say* to draw/A third more opulent than your sisters? *Speak*" (*King Lear* 1.1.94-95, emphasis added). Lear is monstrously, undeniably needy, because he needs not just love, but needs to be able to talk about how his daughters talk about their love for him—a sort of perverse glossophilia? And this focus on language is borne out throughout many characters and scenes: Kent's bluntness and feigned formality, Cordelia's inability to speak at first, the Fool's shocking candor, Edgar's finding a "voice" through his harrowing ordeals, Lear himself speaking very differently as the play progresses, all the evil characters' ability to use and manipulate language, while the good characters begin by misunderstanding and miscommunicating. Again, the similarity to *Confessions* (or, without claiming the mantle of "Augustine scholar," I would say throughout Augustine's thought) is striking. Ironically, despite being the author from antiquity with the most surviving words available to us, Augustine evaluates language as one of the most diseased and contagious parts of human life, thoroughly infected by sin. When he recounts the transition from inarticulate infancy, to a child capable of making himself understood, while understanding others, he does not present it as a happy and liberating evolution or improvement that would better connect him to his fellows, but rather a calamitous drowning deeper and further in sin and oppression, as he "waded deeper into the stormy world of human life" (*Conf.* 1.8.13). The poignancy in either text is tragic and compelling, as we will see in Chapter 2.

Still in Act 1, I am struck by how perceptive and sympathetic Edmund is in his "Thou, Nature, art my goddess" soliloquy (*King Lear* 1.2.1), and alerted by that speech, how much we then see that every character has something to say about "Nature/nature." And of course, the staging itself implies an idea of "Nature," that the physical, meteorological storm is another manifestation of the inner, psychological or spiritual turmoil Lear is suffering. And that "pathetic fallacy" I think is not just a quaint personification or literary device, but shows us that Shakespeare is thinking of both kinds of "nature"–"natural" as opposed to artificial, the natural world outside of us, that we try to understand, manipulate, and dominate; and "human nature," the nature that is within us and guides us (and which also might be difficult or painful for us to understand). Here again, while Augustine is not as explicit or emphatic as Shakespeare, he has left hints of the same ideas. His repudiation of astrology in Book VII is perfectly in accord with Edmund's complaint (if not his evil actions). And letting the analysis run now in both directions: *King Lear* has a good claim to being one of the most vivid, horrible enactments of characters who give Augustine's *libido dominandi* full reign to deceive, murder, mutilate, and torture one another. Both senses of "nature" in both texts will occupy us in Chapter 3.

Finally, we will examine reason in both these texts, which help us understand how they are thinking of humans, by the way they closely associate reason with "nature." This is done most dramatically in Lear's last speech before we find him in the storm (and one that I always observe closely in a production, as I think the actor's handling of it is more crucial than how he/she handles the storm speeches): "O, reason not the need! ... Allow not nature more than nature needs,/Man's life is cheap as beast's" (*King Lear*, 2.4.304, 306-07). In both texts, reason is considered a vital way to understand the natural world: astrology is not just wicked or impious, it is profoundly silly, and reason can disprove it. But reason is rejected by both as the constitutive or definitive element of human nature: everything Goneril and Regan do is "reasonable" at some level (and hence Lear's anguished cry, above), but it is also clearly inhuman and monstrous. The two texts part ways (as they will in our final chapter) with how they conceive the alternative to reason. In *King Lear* it is associated with madness (especially the Fool's antics, then Lear's more anguished speeches), as Edgar diagnoses it, "Reason in madness" (*King Lear*, 4.6.193), which is associated with the rejection of the dehumanizing society in which they live. And while I see that description as broad enough to include being a "fool for Christ" that St. Paul would speak of, the play is never explicit in its endorsement of such[9]: there is something divine or spiritual going on throughout the play, and this is decidedly non-rational, but it seems to be more at home with a kind of pantheism, than any kind of monotheism.[10] Augustine, of course, comes to reject the inhumane, impious society of the Late Roman Empire and his (and his parents', even his pious mother's) aspirations to succeed in such a world, but for him the only alternative is devotion to the mysterious, countercultural, but (he believes) very much available, God of Abraham, Isaac, and Jacob.

Our last chapter considers all these points, and the resolution Augustine finds in God and with fellow believers, made most vivid in the vision at Ostia with his mother. But there can be nothing similar in a tragedy: *King Lear* gestures toward very brief, fleeting experiences similar to that of Augustine and Monica at Ostia, but it simply cannot traffic in anything like the happy ending of *Confessions* (contra the Tate version that gives *King Lear* exactly that, much to the horror of Shakespeare fans like the current author): "The play is a storm, with no subsequent clearing."[11] The point of tragedy is for us to experience the characters' pain, not to see it assuaged, and not even to learn morals or lessons from it, and this was exactly Augustine's (and Plato's) condemnation of it: "In the capacity of spectator one welcomes sad feelings; in fact, the sadness itself is the pleasure. What incredible stupidity!" (*Conf.* 3.2.2). Condemnation is not our goal, however, but appreciation that these two texts together have given us a fuller experience of the tragedies implicit in love, language, nature, and reason.

Throughout my presentation, I assume a basic familiarity with both works, and a more than basic interest in knowing more (perhaps even an unusually high level of devotion to both texts); I cannot imagine one would have bought a book like this if one had read neither of the two texts I proposed putting in dialogue with one another (and with the reader), and developed an abiding interest in them. I will, however, along the way remind readers of the details in a particular scene or passage I'm analyzing, as I know I myself often have to look up what Kent's name was while in disguise, or how many years Augustine was with his son's mother.

Let us begin this journey through these two masterworks. I at least believe one finds in them that quality Augustine cries out to and praises in God—"Beauty so ancient and so new" (*Conf.* 10.27.38).

Notes

1 Cf. Margaret R. Miles, *Augustine and the Fundamentalist's Daughter* (Eugene, OR: Cascade Books, 2011), 3, where she similarly describes how her book "seeks to demonstrate that rereading the same text—the right text—across a lifetime can give form and articulation to ideas and experiences that would otherwise seem to be *spilled and scattered* without meaning or significance (11.29). When one brings the question of *oneself* to reading, rereading, rethinking, reinterpreting the same text at different ages, in different circumstances, and with different heated interests, new understandings occur—especially, gradually, the understanding that the missing self was always right there, right here" (emphasis in original). Similarly in her conclusion, Miles, *Augustine and the*

Fundamentalist's Daughter, 204: "Juan de Valdes, sixteenth-century author of *The Spiritual Alphabet*, wrote, 'In everything you fear and love, closely observed, you will discover yourself.'"

2 Cf. the beautiful appraisal of Miles, *Augustine and the Fundamentalist's Daughter*, 11: "Augustine wrote about books and teachers, but the vividness and accuracy of autobiography depends on showing how, in the exceedingly complex mixture of family, friends, and experiences, the author's ideas were built, bit by bit. For we do not 'have' ideas; we make them and, in turn, the ideas we make, make us. Autobiography is truthful, not by meticulous exposure of all the details of one's life, but by insight. Augustine's *Confessions* is a model of achieving a balance between description of experience and reflection on it."

3 Cf. Carl G. Vaught, *The Journey toward God in Augustine's Confessions. Books I–VI* (Albany, NY: State University of New York Press, 2003), 104: "Yet contrary to what many interpreters suggest, he does not believe that spatiotemporal existence is inherently negative, but that it becomes so as a result of the fall."

4 Miles, *Augustine and the Fundamentalist's Daughter*, 117: "A close reading of the contexts in which Augustine advocated humility indicates that by it he meant something like receptivity, an intellectual and emotional posture inviting learning, an attentiveness in which others' perspectives are generously entertained, listening not for what the author *said*, but for what she *meant*. Augustine's 'humility' is about getting over oneself sufficiently to be free to be attentive to other people and the world" (emphasis in original).

5 I am using the Folger Shakespeare online throughout—https://shakespeare.folger.edu/shakespeares-works/king-lear/

6 Cf. Harold Bloom, *Shakespeare: The Invention of the Human* (New York: Riverhead Books, 1998), 487: "The implicit critique of love, by Shakespeare, hardly can be termed a mere skepticism .... There is love that can be avoided, and there is a deeper love, unavoidable and terrible, far more central to Shakespeare's invention of the human."

7 E.g., Bloom, *Shakespeare*, 503: "Iago has strong passions, however negative. Edmund has no passions whatsoever, he has never loved anyone, and he never will."

8 Cf. Bloom, *Shakespeare*, 508, with similar descriptions of Lear himself: "Lear, however, seems incapable of repressing anything whatsoever. He is simply, by light years, the most violent expressionist in all Shakespeare."

9 Cf. Bloom, *Shakespeare*, 493, on "the fool" as important for understanding the play, but not in any Christian sense: "At once the least secular and yet the least Christian of all Shakespeare's plays,

Lear's tragedy shows us that we are all 'fools', in the Shakespearean sense, except for those among us who are outright villains. 'Fools' in Shakespeare can mean 'dupes', 'beloved ones', 'madmen', 'court jesters', or most of all, 'victims'." On the other hand, Piero Boitani, *The Gospel according to Shakespeare*, translated by Vittorio Montemaggi and Rachel Jacoff (Notre Dame, IN: University of Notre Dame Press, 2013), 30, does make the connection to Paul, that Lear is "following the model outlined by Paul: 'Do not deceive yourselves. If you think that you are wise in this age, you should become fools so that you may become wise. For the wisdom of this world is foolishness with God. For it is written "He catches the wise in their craftiness' (1 Cor. 3:18-19).""

10 Cf. Boitani, *Gospel according to Shakespeare*, 2: "From the second part of *Hamlet* onwards, Shakespeare is meditating on providence, on forgiveness, and on goodness and happiness, and is doing so in Christian terms." Bloom, *Shakespeare*, 493, is at the other extreme: "Faith is absurd or irrelevant in regard to this dark vision of reality .... You have to be a very determined Christianizer of literature to take any comfort from this most tragic of all tragedies." A little later he seems a bit closer to my position that *King Lear* is compatible with a Christian worldview (like that of *Confessions*), though he would say this is irrelevant: "You can deny the pragmatic nihilism of *King Lear* or *Hamlet* if you are a firm enough theist, but you will be rather beside the point, for Shakespeare neither challenges nor endorses your hopes for a personal resurrection" (Bloom, *Shakespeare*, 506). His dismissal of such sounds much more bitter a few pages earlier, urging us to cast "aside irrelevant transcendental moralizings" (Bloom, *Shakespeare*, 486). For Bloom, you might as well note that the physical curtain that comes down at the performance you just saw is blue, and blue is your favorite color: this is at best a distracting coincidence, utterly irrelevant to the play, and more probably, one that proves you did not do a very good job of watching the play, if that's the main thing you observe about it.

11 Bloom, *Shakespeare*, 493. Cf. his earlier dismissal of the Tate version: "His nihilizing madness matters to us, and his restored sanity does not, since true poetry indeed is the Devil's party, in William Blake's dialectical sense of the Devil. Nahum Tate's sanitized *King Lear*, with its happy ending of Cordelia married to Edgar, and Lear benignly beaming upon his daughter and his godson, cheered up Dr. Johnson but deprives us of the *kenoma*, the sensible emptiness or waste land in which the actual play by William Shakespeare concludes" (Bloom, *Shakespeare*, 14).

1

The Problem of Love

Though it is Lear's line, "Which of you shall we say doth love us most" (*King Lear* 1.1.56), that moved me to start this analysis with love, that is not the first or most shocking line about love in the play. I noted the play is different in many ways from other tragedies, and we should specify some of that here at the beginning, even as we discover more as we go. The play violates many of the conventions of dramaturgy; since Shakespeare surely knew these rules and usually followed them, then the flouting of them here seems deliberate, though its intention or effect is not as certain. One of the ways the play deviates from the norm is in its inclusion of a parallel or double plot, as many difficulties as this raise in staging the play—so many that (for this and many other reasons) a critic far above my station simply and finally dismisses the project of ever putting the play on stage: "I have attended many stagings of King Lear, and invariably have regretted being there."[1] The play is not just about Lear and his daughters, it is about Gloucester and his sons, and their conflicts are similar, and somehow meant to illuminate each other. This results in other deviations to support the double plot—e.g., the inclusion of more characters, which can be taken as a distraction from or dilution of the impact the main plot can have on the audience.[2]

This immediately shapes our discussion of love in the play, because the characters of the parallel plot, Gloucester and Edmund, actually appear and speak before the more regal and spectacular entrance of Lear and his daughters. And their relationship and how they speak of it show some deep problems with love. Here is the earl of Gloucester, introducing his illegitimate son, Edmund, to the earl of Kent:

KENT
Is not this your son, my lord?

GLOUCESTER
His breeding, sir, hath been at my
charge. I have so often blushed to acknowledge
him that now I am brazed to 't.

KENT
I cannot conceive you.

GLOUCESTER
Sir, this young fellow's mother could,
whereupon she grew round-wombed and had indeed,
sir, a son for her cradle ere she had a husband
for her bed. Do you smell a fault?

KENT
I cannot wish the fault undone, the issue of it
being so proper.

GLOUCESTER
But I have a son, sir, by order of law,
some year elder than this, who yet is no dearer in
my account. Though this knave came something
saucily to the world before he was sent for, yet was
his mother fair, there was good sport at his making,
and the whoreson must be acknowledged.

(*KL* 1.1.8-24)

These lines add further ways in which they subvert expectations and violate rules, as they have begun the tragedy on a note of bawdy humor, with Gloucester clearly making Kent uncomfortable at his offhand, cavalier joking about adultery, and Kent trying to deflect it or wrench the conversation back into a more decorous direction by complimenting Edmund.

And to return to my observations about teaching the play so many times, I would note that until recently, I do not think I got much beyond acknowledging these lines' inappropriate tone, and thinking they were an apt introduction to Gloucester, who seems a well-meaning but sometimes ridiculous character in the play,[3] not really capable of or interested in the deeper experiences and theorizing of Lear:

> A drama so comfortless succeeds because we cannot evade its power, of which the largest element is Lear's terrible greatness of affect. You can deny Lear's authority, as some now do, but you still must apprehend that in him the furnace comes up at last. Nothing I know of in the world's literature, sacred or secular (a distinction this play voids), hurts us so much as Lear's range of utterances .... You can fail to perceive Lear's greatness, if your program does not allow for such a quality's existence. But then, who or what are you, if you lack even the dream of greatness?[4]

Lear is gigantic in the worst but most compelling ways of mind and heart. Gloucester, on the other hand, is introduced and remains for some time, more instinctive and impulsive in both his vices (casual, openly acknowledged adultery) and his virtues (standing up for Lear when the ugliness of what is being done to him offends Gloucester at some deep level of feeling and compassion, not thought or justice). I have heard too much recently from politicians who say they trust their gut, but I almost think in the case of Gloucester, we see the best case version of that—a man whose shortcomings and thoughtlessness harm his personal life, but who in his dealings with people outside his family has basically good urges and is dedicated and reliable in pursuing them. But the more I taught the play, the more I saw the lines from Edmund's point of view. We begin the play with a character being humiliated in public, and whether or not Edmund shows he is "brazed" to this kind of treatment (or pretends to be) is an important choice for the actor. But inured or not, there is no amount of therapy that could fix the harm done by having to listen to your father brag about how good your mother was in bed—and do so *in front of strangers*. (And if Edmund shows he has been "brazed" to it, then that would be from repeated instances of this public abuse.) The boundaries violated by Gloucester and the damage to Edmund are blatant, even if Gloucester presents it as a vulgar but harmless comment.

However, none of this is presented as deliberate cruelty or animosity on Gloucester's part. As he says, Edgar is "no dearer" to him than Edmund (i.e., Edmund is very dear to him), and he has "acknowledged" him and taken responsibility for him. Gloucester is an uncouth reprobate, but he's not a deadbeat dad. But doesn't that make his comments here even worse? If one went around humiliating and degrading people one hated, that could well be a villainous, evil existence, but at least the behavior and affections would match up, as both hostile and harmful. Gloucester makes clear here that he in fact hurts those whom he loves. He also makes clear that his "love" for Edmund's mother has to be put in scare quotes: he was attracted to her physical beauty, he enjoyed her physically, and he physically provides for her child (while seeming oafish and oblivious to that child's emotional or psychological needs). For Gloucester, love seems never to get beyond the physical. Even when he shows great courage in trying to protect Lear, it's to keep him from being physically harmed in the storm. Gloucester is limited to the physical, especially at the beginning of the play.

The degree to which this matches up with Augustine's flawed family relationships in *Confessions* surprises me today, even though I am the one who thought of pairing them. Augustine, like Gloucester, had a son out of wedlock, named Adeodatus. Unlike Gloucester, Augustine was not married to another woman at the time, so neither the liaison nor the child raised as many practical problems for him as they did for Gloucester and his family, but Augustine's analysis of his own urges aligns him closely with Gloucester's even more unrestrained appetites. I state emphatically here at the beginning that the standard student summary (drummed into them by teachers somewhere, I suppose, or dreamed up by mostly male students forced to read the book while too embroiled in puberty themselves), that Augustine was some kind of sex addict, is wildly exaggerated, to say the least.[5] He in fact lived with and was sexually exclusive with his son's mother for fourteen years. But his analysis of himself is that for too many years of his young adult life, "loving" someone meant "having sex" with her, a vivid example of "love" meaning objectification and use,[6] when by the time he writes *Confessions*, he condemns such as antithetical to real love:

> What was it that delighted me? Only loving and being loved. But there was no proper restraint, as in the union of mind with mind, where a bright boundary regulates friendship. From the

> mud of my fleshly desires and my erupting puberty belched out murky clouds that obscured and darkened my heart until I could not distinguish the calm light of love from the fog of lust. (*Conf.* 2.2.2)

Poignantly and I think significantly, neither Gloucester nor Augustine names the mother of his child: each of these women fulfilled very specific, limited, temporary, physical purposes for the man in the story (i.e., the man's sexual gratification and the inconvenient but accepted production of a child), and that role does not require naming or individuality, because it was so merely physical and fleeting.[7] Very close to how I described Gloucester above, Augustine sees himself as having been trapped, even enslaved by physical urges, so much so that they kept him from devotion to God or proper love of other people. This would explain why he draws the shocking and extreme conclusion that for him to properly devote himself to God, he must give up sexuality completely, and not even pursue it in the "safer," more constrained context of marriage, as he had been assuming up until then, would be his path.

Augustine is a deeper thinker and theorist than Gloucester. (He is a more didactic and direct one than Shakespeare, I would say too—Augustine tells, Shakespeare shows.)[8] So Augustine can expound on further problems of love than the overwhelming "erupting" of male puberty. As he condemns his life a little later in Carthage, Augustine considers another problem of love:

> I was not yet in love, but I was enamored with the idea of love, and so deep within me was my need that I hated myself for the sluggishness of my desires. In love with loving, I was casting about for something to love; the security of a way of life free from pitfalls seemed abhorrent to me, because I was inwardly starved of that food which is yourself, O my God .... Loving and being loved were sweet to me, the more so if I could also enjoy a lover's body; so I polluted the stream of friendship with my filthy desires and clouded its purity with hellish lusts. (*Conf.* 3.1.1)

Augustine remains a bit too narrowly focused on "erupting" in this paragraph, but he has rightly intuited something about being in love with love. That overwhelming infatuation he describes can certainly include blinding sexual desire and lusting to possess and penetrate another's body, but it can also linger and be prolonged way longer than the physical, sexual act, by pining and longing and loving the feeling inside us (ultimately a completely solitary act, and one that demands and offers little), rather than loving another person (which offers but also demands a great deal of us). That he is considering this kind of sinful love as well as "mere" sexual desire is clear from the discussion that follows (*Conf.* 3.2.2-3.3.5), which is not about having sex, but indulging in the feelings stirred up by witnessing theatrical shows.

But as provocatively, Gloucester and Edmund's exchange helps us understand not just Augustine's problem with loving his child's mother, but his problem with loving his own father. Patricius, too, was not faithful to his wife, Augustine's mother (*Conf.* 9.9.19). Augustine's comments on Patricius's noticing that Augustine was growing into a man (*Conf.* 2.3.6) seem to have the same (if not as extreme, and perhaps only noted fully many years later, reflecting on the incident) sense of shame at a worldly, lecherous, misguided father, as is shown in the opening of *King Lear*. But as on several other points, Augustine finds reconciliation (or at least, claims to, if we're being totally accurate and honest) with his wayward father that is denied the characters in *King Lear*.[9] The play starts with a shocking display of humiliation and shame that Gloucester is unable to defuse or heal, because for himself, it's enough just to make light of it; his obtuseness in not realizing that "laughter is the best medicine" does not apply to his son is a big part of his tragedy. And the healing that Augustine claims to have found at the end goes beyond reconciliation with his father—it is a huge part of him forgiving and understanding himself enough that he can present himself to God, accept God's forgiveness, and consider himself, his parents, and all believers to be united in love and service: "Let them [all believers who read this] remember with loving devotion these two who were my parents in this transitory light, but also were my brethren under you, our Father, within our mother the Catholic Church, and my fellow-citizens in the eternal Jerusalem, for which your people sighs with longing throughout its pilgrimage" (*Conf.* 9.13.37).

As I say, once Lear enters, things turn much more serious and dramatic than the (so far) harmless peccadilloes of the earl of Gloucester. The scene with Lear is not an accidental meeting, like Gloucester's, but has been called by the aged king for a purpose:

LEAR
Meantime we shall express our darker purpose.—
Give me the map there. Know that we have divided
In three our kingdom, and 'tis our fast intent
To shake all cares and business from our age,
Conferring them on younger strengths, while we
Unburdened crawl toward death. Our son of Cornwall
And you, our no less loving son of Albany,
We have this hour a constant will to publish
Our daughters' several dowers, that future strife
May be prevented now. The two great princes, France and Burgundy,
Great rivals in our youngest daughter's love,
Long in our court have made their amorous sojourn
And here are to be answered. Tell me, my daughters—
Since now we will divest us both of rule,
Interest of territory, cares of state—
Which of you shall we say doth love us most,
That we our largest bounty may extend
Where nature doth with merit challenge. Goneril,
Our eldest born, speak first.

(*KL* 1.1.37-59)

The request may be absurd—far more absurd than Gloucester's teasing his son in public, which may be just gauche or clueless—but it isn't humorous to anyone. It may be variously hurtful to the three daughters, though not quite in the way Gloucester was to Edmund, as we shall see. But let us unpack the conditions Lear has laid out, before we go right to his demand for a verbal statement of love.

The first thing to note is that the divisions are already drawn on the map. The "contest" Lear proposes is rigged, and is so in such a way that everyone can see. (Or at least it is clear once the first daughter speaks and everyone sees she gets an amount that was already pre-drawn on the map.) It is clear to everyone that if Cordelia goes last, she will get the only part remaining; it doesn't matter what she says.[10] And therefore, it doesn't really matter what the other two say, since the best part is being held by Lear for the third speaker. So Lear can rightly be accused of an absurd demand, but not of giving the allotments based on lying or fawning. If the divisions are already made, and Lear controls the order in which his daughters speak, then he is guilty of playing favorites, and of putting on an absurd spectacle and charade—the outcome of which is clearly foregone, and which seems cruelly designed to demand of his daughters an embarrassing, outrageously public display of something private—but not of rewarding flattery. If anything, he has created a venue in which those who are prone to flattery, or lying in general, can be contained, and may be placated or appeased by giving them enough property. Further, the division of the kingdom itself (setting aside for a moment *how* it is divided) seems motivated by a concern for the common good: "that future strife/May be prevented now" (*King Lear* 1.1.47-48). The "darker purpose" Lear acknowledges is that amidst the joy of a betrothal, some less cheerful, practical matters have to be transacted, and he has decided how those are to unfold. All this together, despite the grotesquery of, "Tell me you love me! Right now! In front of all these people! Go!" should alert us to the shrewd elements of what Lear has set up.

But however clever are the divisions and a staged, public announcement of them, the grotesque emotional element is still the integral part, and what causes the conflict and drives the play. I think Lear in this scene is being a reasonably effective ruler (if prone to bombast, and of course actors and directors can steer our evaluation of him a great deal), but a terrible father, or individual who loves.[11] If Gloucester was wrong to make bad jokes in public about "loving" Edmund or Edmund's mother, Lear is wrong to bring private, personal love into the public arena in such a serious, but especially such a commodified, transactional way, making it part of the showmanship of statecraft: "That we our largest bounty may extend" (*King Lear* 1.1.57).

And as wrong as this may be, the effectiveness of it has to be noted again, so that we may understand Lear (and ourselves). Goneril and Regan give responses and get their parts of the kingdom, without apparent rancor, without raising any objection to why this is being done this way:

GONERIL
Sir, I love you more than word can wield the matter,
Dearer than eyesight, space, and liberty,
Beyond what can be valued, rich or rare,
No less than life, with grace, health, beauty, honor;

As much as child e'er loved, or father found;
A love that makes breath poor, and speech unable.
Beyond all manner of so much I love you.

(*KL* 1.1.60-67)

REGAN
Sir, I am made
Of the self-same metal that my sister is,
And prize me at her worth. In my true heart
I find she names my very deed of love;
Only she comes too short, that I profess
Myself an enemy to all other joys
Which the most precious square of sense possesses,
And find I am alone felicitate
In your dear Highness' love.

(*KL* 1.1.76-84)

I emphasize: Goneril and Regan are surely smart enough to see what is happening, so they know this is all pro forma. They could say anything and it would be enough. That they both indulge in hyperbole, and Regan goes the next outrageous step and states her supposed affections in quasi-incestuous terms ("my very deed of love"—and I have twice seen the play staged with her sitting on Lear's lap and him pawing her),[12] shows more of how they are thinking of and using language, than anything about love, and therefore it will occupy us more in our next chapter. For now, let us just say they play along with words, and Kent is right when he departs this scene that love is found in actions, not words: "And your large speeches may your deeds approve" (*King Lear* 1.1.209-210).[13]

But if any of the daughters could say anything and it would not change the outcome, Goneril and Regan know they cannot say *nothing*. And in that they differ remarkably from Cordelia, who does not play along but challenges the charade:

LEAR
... —Now, our joy,
Although our last and least, to whose young love
The vines of France and milk of Burgundy
Strive to be interessed, what can you say to draw
A third more opulent than your sisters'? Speak.

CORDELIA
Nothing, my lord.

LEAR
Nothing?

CORDELIA
Nothing.

LEAR
Nothing will come of nothing. Speak again.

CORDELIA
Unhappy that I am, I cannot heave
My heart into my mouth. I love your Majesty
According to my bond, no more nor less.

(*KL* 1.1.91-102)

This exchange continues into a reasoned defense of her answer by Cordelia; its analysis will make more sense in our Chapter 4, on the role of reason in the play and *Confessions*. For how it impacts our analysis here, let us note it denies the validity of Lear's demand. He demands his daughters say something. Goneril and Regan comply; they do not thereby show love (because love cannot be shown in words, but deeds), but they do show obedience. Cordelia shows disobedience (at least to the outward command), or even disapproval and denial of the demand,[14] and Lear takes it as a denial of love. It is not—it is only denying that love and obedience are identical, or the one entails the other, when they may not be so closely related. We obey people we do not necessarily love; we love people without obedience necessarily being part of the relationship. And more particularly—we love people, trusting they will not make the kind of inappropriate, absurd demands for obedience that Lear has made here.[15]

Once again, I am surprised at how closely analogous a situation is found in *Confessions*. It is with the death of Augustine's friend in Book Four. The mistaken notion of love there might seem very different, as it is usually characterized as Augustine idolizing his friend, treating him as though he would not die, when it is of course in the nature of human beings that they do (*Conf.* 4.6.11).[16]

And here in *King Lear*, it would seem more like Lear wishes to be idolized by his daughters, not that he idolizes them. But Augustine lets slip one very crucial detail that brings the two scenes very close together. He describes the confusion he felt, when his dying friend briefly rallied, and Augustine tried to joke with him about the death bed baptism he had received:

> How wrong I was; for he rallied and grew stronger, and immediately, or as soon as I possibly could (which is to say at the first moment that he was fit for it, for I did not leave him, so closely were we dependent on each other), I attempted to chaff him, expecting him to join me in making fun of the baptism he had undergone while entirely absent in mind and unaware of what was happening. But he had already learned that he had received it, and he recoiled from me with a shudder as though I had been his enemy, and with amazing, new-found independence warned me that if I wished to be his friend I had better stop saying such things to him. I stood aghast and troubled, but deferred telling him of my feelings in order to let him get better first, thinking that once he was in normal health again I would be able to do what I liked with him. But he was snatched away from my mad designs, to be kept safe with you for my consolation: a few days later the fever seized him anew and he died. And I was not there.

Augustine looked forward to the time when he could "do what I liked with him"—when he could control and demand and force his friend to agree with him. Perhaps not to say, "I love you, Aurelius, more than sun and moon and stars," as Lear demands, but something the friend would be unwilling to say or do, something insincere and untrue to the friend's beliefs and values, but to which Augustine thinks he could force him, in a way that is antithetical to friendship, love, and respect.[17] So the selfish love Lear and Augustine display turns out to have a deep, sinful resemblance. It is, ultimately, another aspect of idolatry. An idol is not just a false deity to which one devotes oneself, and on which one relies too much (cf. Lear, "I loved her most and thought to set my rest/On her kind nursery," *King Lear* 1.1.137-38). An idol is an object one can manipulate and make demands of, because it is not a "real" god.[18] It is not just or especially in the raising up of the human beloved to an immortal status the human does not possess, that makes the love wrong. It is in the objectifying of the beloved as a fount that will pour out all the love and affirmation and agreement one needs or wants, and do so on demand, following entirely the demander's timetable and requirements, not the beloved's—that is what is really depraved in both Lear (in his old age) and Augustine (in his adolescence). And how poignantly parallel that both end with the beloved dead, before he or she can be loved properly, as a subject, a companion, a partner, a person whose needs and ideas and feelings are respected, embraced, and cared for.

But with the character of France, whom we barely get to know beyond these lines, Cordelia finds some of that kind of love, a love for the person herself and not any benefits she offers:

FRANCE
.... Love's not love
When it is mingled with regards that stands
Aloof from th' entire point. Will you have her?
She is herself a dowry.

(*KL* 1.1.275-278)

FRANCE
Fairest Cordelia, that art most rich being poor;
Most choice, forsaken; and most loved, despised,
Thee and thy virtues here I seize upon,
Be it lawful I take up what's cast away.
Gods, gods! 'Tis strange that from their cold'st neglect
My love should kindle to enflamed respect.—
Thy dowerless daughter, king, thrown to my chance,
Is queen of us, of ours, and our fair France.
Not all the dukes of wat'rish Burgundy
Can buy this unprized precious maid of me.—
Bid them farewell, Cordelia, though unkind.
Thou losest here a better where to find.

(*KL* 1.1.290-303)

Cordelia "is herself a dowry ... rich ... choice ... precious," and therefore, "loved." Whereas Lear demanded something from her, France sees something in her—"virtues." And almost oxymoronically, these virtues draw forth from him feelings he admits are "strange," of experiencing both passion and admiration, attraction and care, something he calls "enflamed respect"! It seems to be a passion that cannot be disappointed in the beloved, and a devotion that is not as cold and distant as "duties" (Cordelia's disastrously chosen word to describe her bond to her father, 1.1.107).

Interesting too that France calls upon the "gods" at this point. It's ambiguous what he wants from them—just to call on them to witness his transformation? To thank or acknowledge them for it? Or have they been "neglected[ed]"? (Or does that go back to Cordelia's "virtues" three lines previous?)—but there they are, somehow occurring to him as he tries to understand his "strange" and unexpected love for Cordelia. Augustine, of course, would be singular and much more explicit in his invocation. Still speaking of the love he had for his deceased friend and many others in his youth, he conceives much later that God would have to be another partner to any authentic, human loving relationship:

> This is what we esteem in our friends, and so highly we esteem it that our conscience feels guilt if we fail to love someone who responds to us with love, or do not return the love of one who offers love to us, and this without seeking any bodily gratification from the other save signs of his goodwill. From this springs our grief if someone dies, from this come the darkness of sorrow and the heart drenched with tears because sweetness has turned to bitterness, so that as the dying lose their life, life becomes no better than death for those who live on. Blessed is he who loves you, and loves his friend in you and his enemy for your sake. He alone loses no one dear to him, to whom all are dear in the One who is never lost. And who is this but our God, the God who made heaven and earth and fills them, because it was by filling them that he made them? (*Conf.* 4.9.14)

France can only vaguely gesture toward "gods" as he feels his love for Cordelia grow; Augustine takes the terrible pain of the loss of a friend, and feels the need for God to be there, both to heal the inevitable pain of human relationships, but also to fulfill and guide people in their love, even when it is not being torn apart by mortality. As we will see in our conclusion, this becomes finally a beatific vision for Augustine, only glimpsed and fleeting here on earth, but with the assurance of a permanent enjoyment in the Kingdom. But in the play, it is only a poignant "If only … " in the final scenes with Lear and Cordelia:

LEAR
And take upon 's the mystery of things,
As if we were God's spies. And we'll wear out,
In a walled prison, packs and sects of great ones
That ebb and flow by th' moon.

LEAR
Upon such sacrifices, my Cordelia,
The gods themselves throw incense.
(*KL* 5.3.17-20, 22-24)

Augustine makes necessary and explicit what is only a hope or possibility in *King Lear*: that love between humans is part of their relationship to the gods or God, and that God or gods can be part of relationships—the best and eternal relationships—between people.[19]

Augustine also helps us understand how he is thinking of human love, by describing vividly the joys of it:

> There were other joys to be found in their company which still more powerfully captivated my mind—the charms of talking and laughing together and kindly giving way to each other's wishes, reading elegantly written books together, sharing jokes and delighting to honor one another, disagreeing occasionally but without rancor, as a person might disagree with himself, and lending piquancy by that rare disagreement to our much more frequent accord. We would teach and learn from each other, sadly missing any who were absent and blithely welcoming them when they returned. Such signs of friendship sprang from the hearts of friends who loved and knew their love returned, signs to be read in smiles, words, glances and a thousand gracious gestures. So were sparks kindled and our minds were fused inseparably, out of many becoming one. (*Conf.* 4.8.13)

If these are the joys proffered by a flawed, imperfect, transient human love, then even in its lower form it is a very sensual, intellectual, spiritual, all-consuming consolation of human life indeed, and the full, divinely augmented version must be indescribable in its intensity and ability to transform and uplift. I go back to my earlier characterization of both *King Lear* and *Confessions* as profoundly, exhilaratingly this-worldly books, not about retreating from or denying our personal and emotional entanglements, but reconfiguring, renewing, and rededicating ourselves to them.

Let us focus on one part of Augustine's idea of love and friendship in particular—that the two (or in his description possibly even more, a whole community of lovers) are approaching connection with each other, to the point of unity and identity: "As a person might disagree with himself .... So were sparks kindled and our minds were fused inseparably, out of many becoming one." He notes this identity with his deceased friend, that he was "like another self .... It was well said that a friend is half one's own soul" (*Conf.* 4.6.11), and similarly with Alypius, "my heart's brother" (*Conf.* 9.4.7). This comes out in many scenes in *King Lear* that we will examine in later chapters on nature and reason, but let's take one very early, between Kent, Lear, and the Fool:

FOOL
Sirrah, I'll teach thee a speech.

LEAR
Do.

FOOL
Mark it, nuncle:
Have more than thou showest.
Speak less than thou knowest,
Lend less than thou owest,
Ride more than thou goest,
Learn more than thou trowest,
Set less than thou throwest;
Leave thy drink and thy whore
And keep in-a-door,
And thou shalt have more
Than two tens to a score.

KENT
This is nothing, Fool.

FOOL
Then 'tis like the breath of an unfee'd lawyer.
You gave me nothing for 't.—Can you make no use
of nothing, nuncle?

LEAR
Why no, boy. Nothing can be made out of nothing.

FOOL, *to Kent*
Prithee tell him, so much the rent of his
land comes to. He will not believe a Fool.

LEAR
A bitter Fool!

FOOL
Dost know the difference, my boy, between a
bitter fool and a sweet one?

LEAR
No, lad, teach me.

FOOL
That lord that counseled thee
To give away thy land,
Come place him here by me;
Do thou for him stand.
The sweet and bitter fool
Will presently appear:
The one in motley here,
The other found out there.

LEAR
Dost thou call me "fool," boy?

FOOL
All thy other titles thou hast given away. That
thou wast born with.

KENT
This is not altogether fool, my lord.

(*KL* 1.4.119-155)

As I scanned these, I was struck by how many of Kent's and Lear's lines seemed interchangeable to me, between speakers; the meaning and effect for several lines would not be much changed if the speaker was the other man. Lear treats Kent (in disguise here and following) and the Fool as friends, confidants, and therefore they can tell him what he should be able to observe himself. In these lines and elsewhere, Kent and the Fool can move Lear to accept the "nothing" that in the opening scene sent him into a blinding rage. The Fool can call Lear a fool, and have Kent pretty much endorse the identification, or even a "boy," and Lear again is acquiescent, even jovial. By the next scene, the Fool elicits the crucial confession from Lear, "I did her wrong" (*King Lear* 1.5.24). These are all excellent examples of "tough love," more moving to me than most, which tend too much toward the "tough" and make it hard to see the "love": here and throughout, I feel we have the gentlest, subtlest of chiding, even though the subject itself is "bitter" as Lear recognizes. It is also an excellent illustration of an observation I owe to Harold Bloom and honor him for, that whatever his obvious and titanic faults, Lear is loved by many and very good people in the play:

> When I teach *King Lear*, I have to begin by reminding my students that Lear, however unlovable in the first two acts, is very much loved by Cordelia, the Fool, Albany, Kent, Gloucester, and Edgar—that is to say, by every benign character in the play—just as he is hated and feared by Goneril, Regan, Cornwall, and Oswald, the play's lesser villains.[20]

I think much of understanding the play falls into place once one recognizes this fact. And so interesting and tending to confirm the trustworthiness of the origin of my analysis, that Bloom also notes the source of some of his ideas, like this one, in his teaching of the play. If Lear shocks us with his awful behavior, he comes with an unusually large number of trustworthy character witnesses, and we have to reckon with that as we struggle with his unlikability.

Of course, there is another identity audiences of the play will know well, if they have seen several performances. If two friends grow into identity with one another, as Augustine describes, and we see here even three together completing each other's thoughts with Kent, the Fool, and Lear, then other identities are possible within the loving group: "out of many becoming one." Right before this exchange, we were told the Fool was very fond of and close to Cordelia: "Since my young lady's going into France, sir, the/Fool hath much pined away" (*King Lear* 1.4.73-74). I have seen the opening scene done with the Fool hanging, silently, on Cordelia's sleeves, which is odd in some ways (why doesn't he speak up, like Kent?), but perhaps also very appropriate, given this description of their closeness. So before the events of the play, Cordelia, the Fool, and Lear would have been connected in mutual love and could have had a conversation like that between Lear, the Fool, and Kent.[21] This loving identity is shown when the play is performed with the roles of the Fool and Cordelia played by the same actor, as it often is, and the effect is astonishing. We basically have on stage in the scenes with Lear and the Fool, a recurring reenactment of the confrontation from the opening scene (again cf. the repetition here of "nothing"), and now the Fool's chiding comes across as though it were from Cordelia—and even more importantly, Lear's cheerful acceptance of the reprimand comes across as though he were directing it at his wronged daughter.[22] That is certainly how we experience it, because it's the same actor, and we're constantly wondering how much Lear realizes. As with several other points, it is poignantly reimagined at the end, with Lear's final confusing of the two, when he says of Cordelia's death, "And my poor fool is hanged" (*King Lear* 5.3.369).[23]

To focus on another part of Augustine's description of true friends, he notes friendly disagreements. This is what Lear is most disastrously incapable of at the beginning of the play. When Kent tries direct, undisguised, tough love, and without the Fool's ameliorating presence, it does not end with teaching, learning, or compromise, but with rejection, curses, and the threat of murder:

KENT
Royal Lear,
Whom I have ever honored as my king,
Loved as my father, as my master followed,
As my great patron thought on in my prayers—

LEAR
The bow is bent and drawn. Make from the shaft.

KENT
Let it fall rather, though the fork invade
The region of my heart. Be Kent unmannerly
When Lear is mad. What wouldst thou do, old man?

Think'st thou that duty shall have dread to speak
When power to flattery bows? To plainness honor's bound
When majesty falls to folly. Reserve thy state,
And in thy best consideration check
This hideous rashness. Answer my life my judgment,
Thy youngest daughter does not love thee least,
Nor are those empty-hearted whose low sounds
Reverb no hollowness.

LEAR
Kent, on thy life, no more.

KENT
My life I never held but as a pawn
To wage against thine enemies, nor fear to lose it,
Thy safety being motive.

LEAR
Out of my sight!

KENT
See better, Lear, and let me still remain
The true blank of thine eye.

LEAR
Now, by Apollo—

KENT
Now, by Apollo, king,
Thou swear'st thy gods in vain.

LEAR
O vassal! Miscreant!

ALBANY/CORNWALL
Dear sir, forbear.

KENT
Kill thy physician, and thy fee bestow
Upon the foul disease. Revoke thy gift,
Or whilst I can vent clamor from my throat,
I'll tell thee thou dost evil.

(*KL* 1.1.156-190)

Even at his most direct and confrontational, Kent's love for Lear is overwhelming. And he is explicit and detailed in its implications. The love is toward "father ... master ... patron." He offers "prayers" for his beloved king, but backs these up with concrete actions, even repeatedly risking his own life: "My life I never held but as a pawn/To wage against thine enemies, nor fear to lose it,/ Thy safety being motive." But most of all, Kent shows that loving someone means being truthful with them, even or especially if this means disagreeing with the beloved: "Think'st thou that duty shall have dread to speak/When power to flattery bows? To plainness honor's bound/When majesty falls to folly .... Or whilst I can vent clamor from my throat,/I'll tell thee thou dost evil." Devotion to the beloved entails complete devotion to the truth, even or especially if the beloved does not appreciate the sacrifice.

Exactly as we saw above with France's vague invocation of "gods" when speaking of his newfound love for Cordelia, and how the analogue to that in Augustine contains a very explicit reference to God making fast, secure, and permanent, the loves between finite mortals, so too here we have the tough, truth-telling love of Kent based on "honor," not on any specifically divine inspiration. Kent even includes a denial of Lear's swearing to gods (Apollo). The loves in *King Lear* are explainable in completely and exclusively human terms (if we want to explain them so). But when we turn to *Confessions*, once again the analogous relationship is much more explicit in its devotion to and awareness of God. Who is Augustine's consistent (though by no means infallible), patient truth-teller, who suffers endlessly for him—and thanklessly so until many years after all these sacrifices and trials? Of course it is his mother, Monica. And I think the scene at the end of Book Three is especially analogous, both to Kent's rejected, despised candor, but also nicely and tellingly parallel to Augustine's intellectual bullying of his dying friend in Book Four. With Monica's dream, in which she sees herself standing on a wooden ruler, weeping for her lost son (Augustine deeply immersed at the time in the Manichaean beliefs that Monica eschewed and that by the time he writes *Confessions*, he would also consider heretical and anathema). In the dream, she is consoled by a young man, who tells her to have no more concern or sadness, because where she is now on the ruler, her son would also be. And when she looks next to herself in the dream, there is Augustine.

When Monica relates this dream to Augustine, he says he tried the same kind of specious cajoling or arrogant, authoritative "mansplaining" to a supposedly simple, ignorant woman, that he would later plan to do to his friend. Augustine disrespected his friend, and dishonored their love, by assuming his friend would eventually join him in mocking his baptism, succumb to Augustine's persuading him to repudiate his conversion, and obediently, servilely fall into line with Augustine's "right" beliefs (beliefs Augustine would later regard as utterly wrong and abhorrent). Here he disrespects his mother, and rejects her love, by assuming he can tell her that her dream confirms his Manichaean beliefs, and that it even foretells her conversion to them. Monica more than makes up for not being as rhetorically skilled and trained as her son or his friend, by being much more confident and self-assured than the boys (and, Augustine would insist years later, by being *right* and indeed, right because God was speaking through her):

> Another telling point was that when she had related the vision to me, and I had launched into an attempt to persuade her that she must not give up hope of some day becoming what I was, she promptly replied, without the slightest hesitation, "No: I was not told, 'Where he is, you will be too,' but, 'Where you are, he will be.'" I confess to you, Lord, that, as my memory serves me—and I have often spoken of this episode—I was more deeply disturbed by this answer that came from you through my sharp-eyed mother than by the dream itself. She was not worried by the false interpretation that had come to me so pat, but saw immediately what needed to be seen, as I had not done until she spoke. The dream foretold, so long in advance, the joy in store for this devout woman many years later, and so gave her comfort in her present anxiety. Nearly nine years were to follow during which I floundered in the mud of the deep and the darkness of deception, often struggling to extricate myself but crashing heavily back again. Yet throughout those years my mother, a chaste, God-fearing, sensible widow of the kind so dear to you, though more eager in her hope was no less assiduous in her weeping and entreaty, never at any time ceasing her plangent prayers to you about me. Her pleas found their way into your presence, but left me still wrapped around by the fog, and enveloped in it. (*Conf.* 3.11.20)

"She must not give up hope of some day becoming what I was"—as though that was what was making Monica so sad, that she wanted to be more like Augustine but just could not yet bring herself to such heights of enlightenment (agreement)! Here is the most sinful and solipsistic expression of "love" imaginable, that the beloved is only loved and trusted if he or she can be convinced to turn himself or herself into a copy of the lover. It is a profoundly ugly version of the healthier, more holistic idea of the two loving friends being two halves of a whole (cf. the popular phrasing of "you complete me"), twisted here into one whole (Augustine or Lear) forcibly and imperiously duplicated. Idolatry has gone the final, hateful, deadening steps, not just of manipulating and making demands of the beloved, but trying to mold him or her into oneself, because oneself is the only thing one really loves.

To finish our examination of truth-telling love, let us consider the climactic example of it in *King Lear*. As Kent risked his life to maintain his honor and his devotion to truth, and to express his love for his unappreciative lord, Lear, we find an unnamed servant at the end of Act 3 trying to do the same for Cornwall, who is in the midst of torturing Gloucester:

FIRST SERVANT
Hold your hand, my lord.
I have served you ever since I was a child,
But better service have I never done you
Than now to bid you hold.

REGAN
How now, you dog?

FIRST SERVANT
If you did wear a beard upon your chin,
I'd shake it on this quarrel. What do you mean?

CORNWALL
My villain?
Draw and fight.

FIRST SERVANT
Nay, then, come on, and take the chance of anger.

REGAN, *to an Attendant*
Give me thy sword. A peasant stand up thus?
She takes a sword and runs at him behind; kills him.

FIRST SERVANT
O, I am slain! My lord, you have one eye left
To see some mischief on him. O! *He dies.*

CORNWALL
Lest it see more, prevent it. Out, vile jelly!
Forcing out Gloucester's other eye.
Where is thy luster now?

(*KL* 3.7.88-102)

As Kent began by enumerating his years of faithful service, so too does the servant. So too is he trying to save Cornwall from committing worse sins than he already has, just as Kent tried to do for Lear. And like Kent, the servant's love is not only for his master, but for truth, humanity, even some (very limited at this point—they've already gouged out one of Gloucester's eyes) sense of justice and mercy—or at least, avoidance of further injustice and cruelty. If the servant has loved and faithfully served someone as unhinged as Cornwall, he must be used to scenes of explosive rage and violence, just as Kent and Cordelia must have been inured to Lear's outbursts. But since Cornwall is much further gone in evil, untruth, and sadistic violence, even than Lear was in the opening scene, the outcome is much worse for all involved—the servant dead, Cornwall dying, Gloucester blinded, Regan free to pursue her own lust and thereby undo herself and all the others.

Let us linger on the scene for a moment, to consider its impact, both in the theater and on the page, both dramatically and analytically, how it makes us feel and what it makes us think. On the one hand, I think it shows vividly the rightness and limits of Bloom's claim that the play should never be staged and we should just read it silently to ourselves, bask in its brilliance privately in our minds.[24] Well—yes and no. Again, I cannot claim to have seen the play enacted enough times to count myself a "real" expert, but I have seen it many times on stage, and I would agree this scene is probably harder to pull off than the storm scenes by which everyone judges a performance and an actor. I would admit that most of the time, this scene is grotesque but laughable, like cartoon violence—and don't even think the Warner Brothers Roadrunner cartoon, but more like "Itchy and Scratchy," the parody version of Tom and Jerry that is featured on *The Simpsons*. So yes, Bloom is on to something: the scene should be the one that most draws us into the action of the play, locks us in an embrace so tight we cannot even imagine escaping the horror of which we are now a part, the evil in which we are now implicated. And yet, most times I have seen it, I have been completely shoved out of the play and firmly back into my "real" life role as spectator, aware of being such, and utterly and pathetically aware of the fictiveness of what is happening, its unreality, maybe even its comic irrelevance to me, like watching professional wrestling on television.

But I mention professional wrestling very deliberately, because any of us who have seen wrestling both on television and also live, in person, can attest to how different is the experience, when done right.[25] A wrestler tied up in the ropes, supposedly being beaten into unconsciousness with a folding, metal chair is laughably amusing on television; in person, surrounded by 60,000 other screaming fans, after ninety minutes of buildup, it is nearly an out of body experience in its intensity.[26] And so too, with I think equal intensity but a lot more depth, here in *King Lear*. I remember the first time I saw it on stage. I went with a friend, who was at that time a professional defense attorney. She had literally, on several occasions, seen brains and blood spattered on walls, inhaled what a dead human body smells like after a few days baking in the summer heat. I wondered how the eye gouging would affect her. Or really, I didn't wonder at all, because I assumed someone used to real-life horrors would be unmoved by any staged enactment of such. The only other times I have had a woman's fingernails driven into my forearm with such force was when I was holding on to my wife's arm as she gave birth to our children (another experience that somewhat exceeds expectations or ideas gleaned from reading or hearing about it). So much for being removed from the action, or just sitting solitarily in the cell of one's imagination to commune with the genius of Shakespeare. My friend and the actors and Shakespeare all worked together perfectly with me that evening to give me a real, abiding sense of pain, hurt, and outrage that my imagination would have never been able to impress so deeply on me, or that I would not remember so clearly now, years later.

And the importance of this scene to the meaning of the play really cannot be overstated. Up until this point, everything after Lear's insane outburst against Cordelia and Kent has favored the evil machinations of Goneril, Regan, Cornwall, and Edmund. The good characters have not yet been able to mount anything of an offense, barely a defense, against their violence and inhumanity. But with this spontaneous, heroic act of a nameless character, out of some kind of devoted love for his evil master, and a sudden, unexpected urge to do good (cf. 4.2.89, where it is said he was "thrilled with remorse"!), everything turns against the evil characters. With Cornwall's death and Regan's liberated lust, all their plans begin to unravel, all their allegiances to one another (based on objectification, instrumentalization, and expediency, not love) disintegrate and erupt into violence directed at one another, and end in mutual (and unfortunately, universal) destruction.

The scene has two important sequels that also further the development of love in the play. Gloucester is informed by Regan, belatedly, of his errors concerning his sons. His response is immediate, full repentance (that takes Lear a bit longer in his plot, as he lingers on the wrongs done him): "O my follies! Then Edgar was abused./Kind gods, forgive me that, and prosper him" (*King Lear* 3.7.111-112). As we saw with love, "gods" are invoked when a character seeks forgiveness. They are also invoked, even more ambiguously, at the very end of the scene, as two other unnamed servants reflect on all the evil that has just transpired, and how they plan to react to it:

SECOND SERVANT
I'll never care what wickedness I do
If this man come to good.

THIRD SERVANT
If she live long
And in the end meet the old course of death,
Women will all turn monsters.

SECOND SERVANT
Let's follow the old earl and get the Bedlam
To lead him where he would. His roguish madness
Allows itself to anything.

THIRD SERVANT
Go thou. I'll fetch some flax and whites of eggs
To apply to his bleeding face. Now heaven help him!
They exit.

(*KL* 3.7.120-129)

"Now heaven help him!"—the servant calls upon "heaven" ("gods"?) to help Gloucester, even as he plans to help him himself. This is part of the beautiful, entrancing ambiguity of the play: the heavens and gods are silent (if they even exist), apparently unmoved or unmovable by all the misery we are forced to witness, but the people who are doing good and noble and loving things, often call upon the gods as they do them. (In our Chapter 3, we will see this again in Lear's transformative speeches.) Are these characters (and Shakespeare's audience) benighted, duped, or lulled by having been raised with such God-talk, and perpetuating such nonsense on to others? My atheist friends would surely say so, and since I am their friend and love them, I would not try to dissuade them or assume they'll come around to my way of regarding this. I cannot call him "friend," as we never met, but it also seems to be Bloom's conclusion, that a pious interpretation here is ridiculous, embarrassing: "Faith is absurd or irrelevant in regard to this dark vision of reality .... That pretty much makes Christianity as irrelevant to *Macbeth* as it is to *King Lear*, and indeed to all the Shakespearean tragedies."[27] But there is nothing in the text that demands this, just as there is nothing there that denies it. Pairing *King Lear* with *Confessions* fits perfectly but not uniquely, I would say, for both texts (despite Augustine's repeated and vehement claims to more certainty) exist in *our* world (or more humbly, we exist in theirs), where God or gods are silent and invisible, but nonetheless intensely present to many of us, when we surprise ourselves with goodness and courage of which we thought ourselves incapable.[28] I would also note this description of calling upon a silent deity while doing what you already know to be right (before or even without the invocation), comports with some recent statements of Pope Francis, who is reported to have said, "You pray for the hungry. Then you feed them. That's how prayer works."[29] It is only the empty, costless and valueless invocation of "Thoughts and prayers," with no costly actions emanating from the sentiment or following on the statement, to which both *King Lear* and *Confessions* would be implacably, constitutionally opposed—and which, at the risk of sounding too didactic here, I would say, rightfully so.[30]

From just a few passages from these two works, we have gleaned significant and connected nuances and implications to the problem of love. From Gloucester and Edmund, we first see that "you always hurt the ones you love," is not just a commonplace, aphoristic observation. We might think, from seeing more of Gloucester and how he bumbles around through life and loves, instinctive but clumsy, that perhaps it is due to some deficiency of character or intellect especially prevalent in (but by no means unique to) him. This is where pairing *King Lear* and *Confessions* has paid off better even than I had hoped. Whatever one might accuse Augustine of, "bumbling" or lack of introspection or analysis would hardly seem apt. (If anything, too intense an obsession with self-analysis and judgment would seem to fit him better.) And yet we see some of the same issues with Augustine as with Gloucester. The young Augustine "loves" people—especially women, most especially the one he cannot even name but which in today's slang would be called his "baby mama"—as Gloucester does, as objects to be used, not subjects to be respected and really loved. If Augustine obsesses and agonizes over this more than Gloucester, that is what shows the differences in their minds and personalities, but the dynamic and urge are the same. Further, as the son of a cheating father, Augustine feels some of the same shame and resentment as Edmund, and it is decades before he comes to some resolution, that loving the imperfect people in one's life is the only option, if one is to love at all. For if one held out for a "perfect," sinless lover or partner, one would never find such a person, and therefore never love. And many of the loves of our lives are not even chosen by us, do not even *appear to be so*, but are relationships into which we are born or placed or thrust (e.g., parents, siblings, children, and colleagues).

Objectification and use or abuse manifest in other ways than sexual attraction, as shown by other loving relationships in both texts. Lear makes demands of his daughters that one should never make of a beloved. He demands they act and speak in a certain way—*his* way—and not from an honesty and spontaneity coming from themselves. He confuses obedience and love, which is to say, he confuses his love with force and power exerted on them, and their love with submission to him. And again, the parallel from *Confessions* shows us this is not just some terrible temptation or expression typical of Elizabethan or ancient British kings, for the young Augustine does much the same to his dying friend, dominating him intellectually, and acting hurt and sullen when the friend rallies his strength and will enough to stand up to and refuse the blasphemous entreaties of his domineering friend, Augustine.

But then we saw in both texts some positive expressions of love. France loved Cordelia for her virtues, not for any use he could make of her (though of course, ironically, that made her very useful indeed as a queen or wife). As he felt this unexpected, unfamiliar love, he mentioned (though only mentioned, not thanked or prayed to) the gods. And when we looked to Augustine, we saw something very similar that friends love each other's virtues, and practice and increase their virtues with each other. Augustine is (understandably) much more explicit that this happens "in God" and the friends' love is cemented and guaranteed and made eternal by its being from, in, and directed to God.

From what Augustine describes of his friendships, even before they achieve the permanence and divine blessing that he thinks they can and should for a faithful lover, we see friends/lovers approaching a community of like-minded, similarly focused and interested, virtuous people, spurring each other on to more learning and virtue. Dramatically, *King Lear* shows this on stage with Lear, Kent, and the Fool (who may also be, or at least remind us of, Cordelia) finishing each others' thoughts, even correcting, reprimanding, or mocking one another. But the limits of this take us to a final problem with love, but one that also shows its ultimate purpose or goal. Kent and Cordelia reprimand Lear to such an extent, and in such a way (publicly, forcefully, and to his warped mind, disrespectfully), that he denies love, threatens hate and violence, and sets in motion events that kill all of them.[31] In Augustine's journey, he was never so dictatorial or solipsistic (or was he just too needy to imagine life without her?), that he would disown his reprimanding, disapproving mother (though he does shamefully flee from her in the night—*Conf.* 5.8.15), but I think Monica's constant weeping for Augustine shows that it was her legitimate and wholly understandable fear for many years that he might perish before they are fully reconciled—which is to say, before he is fully reconciled to the God to whom Monica devotes herself. She thereby shows the real expression and purpose of love: to pursue the truth with the beloved, even or especially if the beloved refuses to. Not in the sense we saw above, of trying to force or command the beloved to do and believe and feel as we do, but by witnessing to the truth to the beloved, no matter how much he rages and threatens against oneself and the truth. The unnamed servant in Act 3 of *King Lear* accomplishes this in a much more dramatic, focused fashion than even Kent, Cordelia, or Monica, by laying down his life for the truth, out of love for it and even for his awful, unworthy master.

Notes

1 Bloom, *Shakespeare*, 476. Cf. also ibid., 512: "Charles Lamb, my precursor in believing that 'Lear is essentially impossible to be presented on a stage', insisted that the greatness of Lear was a matter of intellectual dimension." I am sure I've seen only a small fraction as many productions as Bloom, but I'd be inclined to put it the other way around: every one has been flawed, some profoundly so, but every one has contained something of the most sublime, and something I never would have thought of on my own in solitary reading of the play. Cf. Barry Edelstein, *Thinking Shakespeare: A Working Guide for Actors, Directors, Students... and Anyone Else Interested in the Bard* (rev. ed. New York: Theatre Communications Group, 2018), 430, for a rejection of the idea that staging Shakespeare plays in general is anathema: "There is even a remnant of the eighteenth-century's scholiast's Shakespeare, according to which the theater is nothing more than a distraction from—and a vulgar insult to—the pure literary qualities of the texts. (We theater professionals don't discuss that school of thought in polite company.)" Though Bloom's paean to solitary reading is also worth noting, especially now in a society even more postliterate than when he was writing: "Assaulted by films, television, and computers, our inner and outer ears have difficulty apprehending Shakespeare's hum of thoughts evaded in the mind. Since *The Tragedy of King Lear* well may be the height of literary experience, we cannot afford to lose our capability for confronting it" (Bloom, *Shakespeare*, 476–7).

2 Cf. Bloom, *Shakespeare*, 481, on one of the difficulties raised: "A theatrical answer [to why Gloucester's death is not enacted on stage] might be the intricacies of the double plot already seemed so substantial that Shakespeare declined to risk yet further complexity."

3 Cf. Stephen Booth, "On the Greatness of *King Lear*," in *William Shakespeare's King Lear*, edited by Harold Bloom (New York: Chelsea House, 1987), 57–70, esp. 69: "Gloucester's early speeches

invite their audience to register him as a brutal oaf (an accurate but insufficient estimate)."

4 Bloom, *Shakespeare*, 506, 512.

5 Cf. James J. O'Donnell, *Augustine: A New Biography* (New York: HarperCollins, 2005), 38: "Moderns with the slightest possible familiarity with Augustine's name often think of him obscurely as a paragon of promiscuity.... but nothing suggests he was unusual, and indeed among the privileged young of his time he was probably more rather than less restrained than most."

6 In a different context of love that can go bad (i.e., loving sorrow, esp. the spectacle of sorrow in the theater), Vaught, *Journey toward God in Augustine's* Confessions. *Books I–VI*, 71, makes the same point: "This means that we should not love them for our own satisfaction, but should love them with charity; for only in this way can we express the kind of love that does not simply satisfy our own needs."

7 Cf. O'Donnell, *Augustine*, 39: "She gets short shrift from him, except for a muted pang of guilt expressed years later that still conceals her from our sight, but we would love to know what she made of him."

8 Thus succinctly Maynard Mack, "The World of *King Lear*," in *Twentieth Century Interpretations of King Lear: A Collection of Critical Essays*, edited by Janet Adelman (Englewood Cliffs, NJ: Prentice-Hall, 1978), 56–69, esp. 69: "Tragedy never tells us what to think; it shows us what we are and may be." But on the small scale of individual speeches, there is still a high level of explanation, of argumentation, as explained by Edelstein, *Thinking Shakespeare*, 72: "*Argument*, in the sense that Shakespeare relies on it, is not about heated exchanges, angry disputes, or biting quarrels. Instead, it's about articulating a point of view, stating a position, laying out a line of reasoning, and building a convincing case.... To *argue* is to present a rationale, prove something through reason and logic, and convince someone else of your view" (emphasis in original).

9 Cf. Boitani, *Gospel according to Shakespeare*, 26: "Lear's tragedy is less radical but, paradoxically, more extreme [than Job's].... More extreme, because it is only for a brief moment that Lear is offered restoration: no human or divine blessing saves him from the death of the newly found Cordelia and of Gloucester, or in the end from his own."

10 Cf. Booth, "Greatness of *King Lear*," (1987) 68: "Gloucester and Kent already know the details of the division, and, when Lear invites Cordelia to speak, he has already assigned all of the kingdom but the opulent third reserved for her."

11 Cf. Thomas McFarland, "The Image of the Family in *King Lear*," in *On King Lear*, edited by Lawrence Danson (Princeton, NJ: Princeton University Press, 1981), 91–118, esp. 100: "The tension between

Lear's two roles in life, one as king with its patina of symbolic paternalism, the other as father to a specific family, generates the tragic situation that arises in the play.... Lear pervasively assumes at the outset that his status as king and his status as father are the same, and this initial confusion leads him into the fallacious assumption that power and love are interchangeable." See also Ivor Morris, *Shakespeare's God* (London: Allen and Unwin, 1971), 348, who sees an even more fundamental dichotomy: "This, then, was the terrifying paradox of kingship, which Shakespeare well understood, and to which he gave incomparable expression in *King Lear*: that a king, though a mere man, could not be a king unless he continued to see himself as something more than a man, and to act in accordance with the kingly ideal that conferred a rare kind of mortal divinity upon him."

12 The present author "gets" the staging of Lear grabbing Regan's buttocks—as I say, her lines practically call for such sick, twisted behavior. But I wonder if it's veering too far toward *Fifty Shades of Lear*. And I hope my hesitation is not just my prudishness (though I'm getting used to that in late middle age), but is more about maintaining the mystery of evil in the play. If the Lear girls have been subject to outright incest, their evil is explainable, when the whole experience of the play is that evil is not comprehensible, that it *cannot be* explained in the world of the play (or ours?).

13 Though significantly, even actions require interpretation, as noted in the context of Augustine by Miles, *Augustine and the Fundamentalist's Daughter*, 127: "Similarly, we do not actually *see* love. We see people *acting* in ways we think of as loving, and we (rightly or wrongly) *infer* love" (emphasis in original).

14 Cf. Bloom, *Shakespeare*, 479, 506, noting "Cordelia's recalcitrance in the face of incessant demands for a total love surpassing even her authentic regard for her violently emotional father. Cordelia's rugged personality is something of a reaction formation to her father's overwhelming affection.... It is fascinating that initially Lear attributes Cordelia's recalcitrance to join in her sisters' pompous hyperboles to 'pride, which she call plainness'." See also McFarland, "Images of the Family," 104, who notes that "Cordelia, ... has herself acted with some of the old man's willfulness." Also Rowan Williams, *The Tragic Imagination* (The Literary Agenda; Oxford: Oxford University Press, 2016), 37: "Cordelia (and it is important not to sentimentalize the *prima facie* chill of her response) replies in exactly those terms, almost parodying their crassness."

15 Cf. Williams, *Tragic Imagination*, 37, 40: "What Lear is emphatically not doing is 'divesting' himself of authority in the way he claims, since he controls the currency of the exchange.... The idea that I can dispense or receive love without limit is both the most dangerous of fantasies and the most fundamental of truths; *Lear* is in part about the appalling difficulty of telling the difference between unconditional love as limitless benevolence demanding or earning limitless repayment and unconditional love as that which is always there in advance and never open to negotiation."

16 The description given by Vaught, *Journey toward God in Augustine's* Confessions. *Books I–VI*, 101, is typical and accurate: "When Augustine orients himself toward his friend as if he would never die, he is responding to him as if he were infinite rather than finite; and when this occurs, sin is the inevitable result. Formulated in somewhat different terms, Augustine's relationship with his friend is idolatrous; for in pursuing it, he seeks to derive ultimate satisfaction from one of God's creatures rather than from God himself."

17 Cf. James Wetzel, "Book Four: The Trappings of Woe and Confession of Grief," in *A Reader's Companion to Augustine's Confessions*, edited by Kim Paffenroth and Robert P. Kennedy (Louisville, TN and London: Westminster John Knox, 2003), 53–69: "Seen from another angle, however, it is Augustine's very confidence about what would have happened with his friend that betrays his kind of madness.... Augustine did not of course owe his friend *belief* in the face of his friend's transfiguration, but he did owe it to the friendship not to dismiss out of hand what had elicited his friend's independence of heart and mind. It would have been enough had Augustine been willing to question his own self-certainties before his friend had to die. That is the sort of self-questioning we offer to someone, not out of respect for a superior argument, but out of love" (quotation on 62, emphasis in original).

18 Cf. Vaught, *Journey toward God in Augustine's* Confessions. *Books I–VI*, 26: "God frustrates our attempts to capture him because he is too close to our hearts for us to hold him at a distance and because he is too far from our understanding for him to become a determinate content of cognition."

19 Though cf. Boitani, *Gospel according to Shakespeare*, 4, who thinks the epiphany of God in Shakespeare is fulfilled, and starts with suffering: "In particular, the feeling of the presence of divinity is born initially, in Shakespeare's characters, from pain, from suffering that which is obscure and tragic, and from the experience of death."

20 Bloom, *Shakespeare*, 479.

21 Cf. Bloom, *Shakespeare*, 494: "The exception is the Fool, the uncanniest character in Shakespeare, and the third, with Cordelia and Lear, in the play's true family, its community of love."

22 Cf. James L. Calderwood, "Creative Uncreation in *King Lear*," in *William Shakespeare's King Lear*, edited by Harold Bloom (New York: Chelsea House, 1987), 121–37, esp. 126: "If the same actor

doubled as Fool and Cordelia, then we may see each character embodying merely part of the truth. In the opening scene Cordelia's truth is not 'allowed' and she is banished. But she returns later in the role of the Fool, now 'allowed', and tells Lear the abrasive truth about his own folly."

23 On the identity of the Fool and Cordelia, esp. in that last line, see Stephen Booth, "On the Greatness of *King Lear*," in *Twentieth Century Interpretations of King Lear: A Collection of Critical Essays*, edited by Janet Adelman (Englewood Cliffs, NJ: Prentice-Hall, 1978), 98–111, esp. 104: "The context that dictates that 'fool' refer to Cordelia—Lear's position over her body, the pronoun 'thou', her death by hanging, and the echo of two earlier cycles of grief and hope—coexists with the context provided by a play in which one character is a fool, a professional clown, who has vanished noiselessly during Act III, and by a scene punctuated with six reports of off-stage deaths. Moreover, the syntactic habit of the word 'and' is to introduce material relatively extraneous to what precedes it.... Here again, one sentence, 'And my poor fool is hanged', makes two distinct and yet inseparable statements Our minds are firmly fixed in two places at once." Also Harold C. Goddard, "*King Lear,*" in *William Shakespeare's King Lear*, edited by Harold Bloom (New York: Chelsea House, 1987), 9–43, esp. 34: "His wandering mind has confused them, if you will. But what a divine confusion! Has *wedded* them would be the better word. Think how the Fool loved his master! Think how he adored Cordelia and pined away after she went to France!"

24 Bloom, *Shakespeare*, 476–7.

25 Cf. the still classic analysis of Roland Barthes, "The World of Wrestling," in *Mythologies* (New York: Hill and Wang, 1972), 15–25.

26 I am not a regular attendee, but I refer here to Wrestlemania VIII, Indianapolis, April 5, 1992, where I saw, and was utterly convinced with a ferocity beyond any religious zealotry, that Hulk Hogan was immobilized and about to be beaten to death (or worse) by Sid Vicious and Papa Shango. When the Ultimate Warrior's theme music blared and he raced to the ring to save Hulk, I both knew I was really alive and thought I would die. I had a headache for two days after.

27 Bloom, *Shakespeare*, 493, 521.

28 Cf. William C. Hackett, "'And Thou, all-Shaking Thunder…' A Theological Notation to Lines 1–38 of *King Lear*, Act III, Scene II," *Religions* 8 (5) (2017): 91; online at https://doi.org/10.3390/rel8050091: "If not Christian, neither is Lear's curse on humanity and the world exactly pagan: Greek tragedy turns on the reconciliation of humanity with its own mortality, under the unconquerable enigma of the will and purpose of the immortal gods."

29 The quotation is all over the internet (e.g., http://iym.ptsem.edu/how-prayer-works/), without any attempt to locate when or where it was first said.

30 Prayers to an assumed God are compared to the brutality of the play's villains by Julian C. Rice, "The Empathic Edgar: Creativity as Redemption in *King Lear*," *Studia Mystica* 7 (1984): 50–60, esp. 53: "It is as unrealistic to expect to ensure the future through violent brutality as through praying to a virtue rewarding God."

31 I am taking Kent's line, "I have a journey, sir, shortly to go;/My master calls me. I must not say no" (*King Lear* 5.3.381-82), as a reference to an imminent, planned suicide.

2

The Problem of Language

As noted in Chapter 1, the opening scene of *King Lear* frames the problem of love as somehow (at least in this case) also a problem of language. Although it is natural to rephrase the conflict as Lear wanting his daughters to display their love for him, he phrases it differently than that: "Which of you shall we say doth love us most,/ ... speak" (*King Lear* 1.1.56, 59). Lear commands (verbally) them to say something about which he can then speak: there are at least three speech acts (multiplied by three daughters!), and there seems to be far more about language, really, than feeling, in his request and in what follows on it. And their responses, though ostensibly about love, expressed in language, turn out to be just as much about the medium as the message, to reveal very different ideas about how language works, or even what it is for, ultimately.

To dissect what goes on with language in what follows, we should consider where the characters seem to agree and disagree, in their use and evaluation of language. Let us examine first how parallel are parts of Goneril and Cordelia's speeches:

GONERIL
Sir, I love you more than word can wield the matter, ...
A love that makes breath poor, and speech unable.
Beyond all manner of so much I love you.

(*KL* 1.1.60, 66-67)

CORDELIA, *aside*
What shall Cordelia speak? Love, and be silent.

CORDELIA, *aside*
Then poor Cordelia!
And yet not so, since I am sure my love's
More ponderous than my tongue.

CORDELIA
Unhappy that I am, I cannot heave
My heart into my mouth.

(*KL* 1.1.68, 85-87, 100-101)

If language is just a neutral way to transmit ideas from one person to another, there should be no difference in reaction to these lines, because the ideas they convey are identical: both women are claiming that language is insufficient for expressing their love. Further, they both seem to imply this is not because of the meagerness of language, but because of the immensity of their love.

But Lear shrugs off Goneril's response as pro forma, expected but unimportant, and rewards it according to the rules of the "game" he has established, while Cordelia's response sends him into a murderous, uncontrollable rage.[1] So language is not just a vessel in which ideas fly from one person to another, with the ideas being the important part of the transmission.[2] Perhaps a mathematical equation means the same thing no matter who says it, or when, or where, or to whom, but any statement of a more personal nature, relies on all these factors for its meaning and effect. As noted, Goneril's statement (or something similar to it) is expected by Lear, so her words have no weight, really. Cordelia's speech is utterly unexpected, and in the case of the final lines just quoted, only comes after "Nothing" has been said four times, before she can make a fuller statement. Again: given the situation he has set up, Lear is not succumbing here to flattery, but exploding at insubordination. As noted in Chapter 1, Cordelia has challenged Lear in a way that Goneril has not at all (in this scene—she will only challenge her father later, when she's convinced she can destroy or subjugate him completely). And as Cordelia's asides show, her challenge seems to come from an overwhelming, inconsolable hurt and outrage at this public demand and display. (Since she is able to express her feelings privately in the asides, it is not a matter of her lacking feeling, even though that is how her father foolishly interprets it.)

From similar statements of the incommensurability of language and feeling, Cordelia and Goneril draw wildly different conclusions, of course. Given the rest of the play, Goneril clearly believes that because language and feeling needn't coincide, and any mature adult should be aware of that situation, then one is free to say anything advantageous under the circumstances. If anything, language is the primary category: for a social and political animal such as she, one decides first on how to present oneself to the outside world—perfect wife, sister, daughter, duchess, lady, in this case—and proceeds to make statements in accord with that image. If feelings match up with the assumed role or persona, or utterly contradict it, is then only a matter of the power that the speaker is then wielding. As noted above, when Lear is sufficiently isolated and weakened, Goneril's language changes, from fawning to insulting, demanding, and demeaning:

GONERIL
Not only, sir, this your all-licensed Fool,
But other of your insolent retinue
Do hourly carp and quarrel, breaking forth
In rank and not-to-be-endurèd riots. Sir,
I had thought by making this well known unto you
To have found a safe redress, but now grow fearful,
By what yourself too late have spoke and done,
That you protect this course and put it on
By your allowance; which if you should, the fault
Would not 'scape censure, nor the redresses sleep
Which in the tender of a wholesome weal
Might in their working do you that offense,
Which else were shame, that then necessity
Will call discreet proceeding.

(*KL* 1.4.206-219)

Words can indeed wield the matter, when you now have the power to tell your father he's a senile, old fool, without fear of punishment or reprisal, and your previous lack of power was all that was keeping you from saying just that. The same when you no longer need pretend to respect your spouse as he opposes your evil plans:

GONERIL
Milk-livered man,
That bear'st a cheek for blows, a head for wrongs;
Who hast not in thy brows an eye discerning
Thine honor from thy suffering; that not know'st
Fools do those villains pity who are punished
Ere they have done their mischief. Where's thy
drum?
France spreads his banners in our noiseless land,
With plumèd helm thy state begins to threat,
Whilst thou, a moral fool, sits still and cries
"Alack, why does he so?"

ALBANY
See thyself, devil!
Proper deformity shows not in the fiend
So horrid as in woman.

GONERIL
O vain fool!

ALBANY
Thou changèd and self-covered thing, for shame
Bemonster not thy feature. Were 't my fitness
To let these hands obey my blood,
They are apt enough to dislocate and tear
Thy flesh and bones. Howe'er thou art a fiend,
A woman's shape doth shield thee.

GONERIL
Marry, your manhood, mew—

(*KL* 4.2.62-83)

And the same, finally, when you think you have the power to openly carry on adultery—then there's no reason to hide it with words or any other subterfuge: "Say if I do; the laws are mine, not thine./ Who can arraign me for 't?" (*King Lear* 5.3.189-190). For Goneril, the disconnect between language and any feelings or ideas is really just a temporary accident of the weak, who have to watch their language carefully, so as not to alert or provoke the strong. But it is a very useful situation nonetheless, because the outward language can then be used like any stealth, deception, or trap is used by a cunning predator.

But for Cordelia, the disconnect between outward language and inner thoughts and feelings seems much more fundamental, precisely because she is so sincere throughout. (As noted, there isn't much insincerity or disconnect, for Goneril, once she's achieved the power to destroy anyone who doesn't like what she's saying or doing.) There is never any concern on her part that her language may harm her. (Some concern is expressed in her asides, but I don't think it need be taken as fear for her own safety.) If anything, there is only incredulity that her father cares so much for language as to even ask such a thing, because feelings and the actions that proceed from them are all that matter, according to her. But this idealism comes at a price. If language is so disconnected from feelings, and feelings are the primary category and the one that needs urgently to be communicated and shown, then she feels compelled to say the antagonistic—yes, even hubristic, I feel—"Nothing."[3] And when she tries to explain this compulsion a few lines later, the pride is much more palpable, and expressed much more eloquently:

> CORDELIA, *to Lear*
> I yet beseech your Majesty—
> If for I want that glib and oily art
> To speak and purpose not, since what I well intend
> I'll do 't before I speak—that you make known
> It is no vicious blot, murder, or foulness,
> No unchaste action or dishonored step
> That hath deprived me of your grace and favor,
> But even for want of that for which I am richer:
> A still-soliciting eye and such a tongue
> That I am glad I have not, though not to have it
> Hath lost me in your liking.
>
> (*KL* 1.1.257-268)

Boldly she asserts her actions speak for her, not words ("To speak and purpose not, since what I well intend/I'll do 't before I speak"). More outrageously, she claims she is "richer" and "glad" she is the way she is, making it clear she believes Lear is totally in the wrong (never mind her sisters, whom she's already called out as liars,

1.1.109-115). What we saw in Chapter 1, about love demanding a devotion to the truth, here is shown as making language a contemptible, incoherent mess, to the one devoted to the truth.[4] Whereas many of us would compromise somewhat, say something, feign some contrition, Cordelia thinks language as epitomized by her sisters' use of it is so debased and debasing that she just refuses to participate (except, as here, when it suits her purposes of asserting her own innocence—an accurate enough assertion, and totally sincere, but interesting that she gets more eloquent when trying to defend herself, but is silent or tongue-tied when being asked to obey or at least humor her father. Perhaps even for Cordelia, the degree to which language is irretrievably unusable varies with the context and situation). Cordelia expresses an extreme, inflexible view of language as simply and completely incompatible with truth or love, which for her can only be expressed in silent actions. I have often taught the play soon after Sophocles's *Antigone* and I think the two women are similarly idealistic, inexorably driven to action and implacably repulsed by "mere" words.

From similar statements of language being incommensurate with feelings or thoughts, Goneril and Cordelia end up at opposite extremes. For Goneril, language is devoid of meaning but therefore very useful, and should be carefully and cynically deployed whenever necessary. For Cordelia, language is devoid of meaning, but this then demands an idealistic silence—or at most, a two-syllable denial of its use: "Nothing," which is short for, "I can/will say nothing, because there's no point." Between these two extremes, Kent and Lear speak in this opening scene with some sense of language being simultaneously inadequate, but also necessary, some sense that it communicates, but always imperfectly, but this is no reason to either abandon or misuse it.

As a way to understand what might be the right use of language, consider Kent's bluntness, to which he himself draws attention:

KENT
… Be Kent unmannerly
When Lear is mad. What wouldst thou do, old man?
Think'st thou that duty shall have dread to speak
When power to flattery bows? To plainness honor's bound
When majesty falls to folly. Reserve thy state,
And in thy best consideration check
This hideous rashness. Answer my life my judgment,

Thy youngest daughter does not love thee least,
Nor are those empty-hearted whose low sounds
Reverb no hollowness.

(*KL* 1.1.162-173)

He admits he is "unmannerly" and "plain," and he connects his own words in support of Cordelia's "low sounds." Kent claims words expressed thusly come from "duty," "honor," "judgment," and most of all, "love." Such blunt speech stands in contrast to "flattery," which only comes from someone who is "empty-hearted" and "hollow." Kent seems to have as much revulsion for Goneril's and Regan's use of language, as did Cordelia. Like her, he condemns such misuse of language as not matching up with an inner disposition, one that is in fact the opposite of what is coming out of the speaker's mouth. But Kent seems to see this as detectable in the outward trappings of such deceitful language (and therefore his real outrage is reserved for Lear, for being so willfully blind as not to detect it, not toward the evil daughters, who are behaving true to form). And therefore, unlike Cordelia, he sees it as the responsibility of truthful people to speak up, not fall silent. If sycophants give themselves away with their ostentatious, overblown speech, then truthful people must mark their speech with "unmannerly ... plainness" to show its sincerity.

But Lear's murderous outburst, resulting in Kent's banishment under pain of death, causes Kent to change tactics, at least outwardly. When Kent reappears in disguise, he underlines that speech must be a part of this subterfuge:

KENT
If but as well I other accents borrow
That can my speech diffuse, my good intent
May carry through itself to that full issue
For which I razed my likeness. Now, banished Kent,
If thou canst serve where thou dost stand condemned,
So may it come thy master, whom thou lov'st,
Shall find thee full of labors.

(*KL* 1.4.1-8)

It is a shrewd and fascinating compromise Kent has now made. The speech games of a Goneril are now to be used carefully—"I other accents borrow/That can my speech diffuse"—and must even be combined with visual, physical deception as well—"I razed my likeness." Goneril is right that the weak must use deception or be destroyed by the powerful. But Kent proposes to use it for wholly different ends, not to benefit and enrich himself, but to bring about "good intent" for his "master." Further, he is doing this out of devotion to one he "lov'st."[5] For Kent it is definitely not a way to say one thing and do another, as it is for Goneril, but to use language to allow him safely to "serve" and perform many "labors," and it is in actions that truth is expressed, so language must be used to make such actions possible and effective. How he introduces himself to Lear when he is in disguise is completely honest and accurate at some level:[6]

KENT
I do profess to be no less than I seem, to serve
him truly that will put me in trust, to love him that
is honest, to converse with him that is wise and says
little, to fear judgment, to fight when I cannot
choose, and to eat no fish.

LEAR
What art thou?

KENT
A very honest-hearted fellow, and as poor as the
King.

LEAR
If thou be'st as poor for a subject as he's for a
king, thou art poor enough. What wouldst thou?

KENT
Service.

LEAR
Who wouldst thou serve?

KENT
You.

(*KL* 1.4.14-26)

If language only obscured intent, as Goneril seems to believe, then Kent might use his disguise and partly deceitful language to gain access to his estranged master so he could kill him. But for Kent, language can be deceptive as to outward appearances, and yet totally truthful in its inner meaning, and benign or even loving in its purpose.

If Kent's candor provoked Lear to "folly" and "hideous rashness," it is even more significant how it affects the villains of the play. To Oswald, Goneril's evil but craven henchman, Kent gives his completely open, frank evaluation, in a particularly impressive fusillade of Shakespearean insults:

KENT
I love thee not.

OSWALD
Why then, I care not for thee.

KENT
If I had thee in Lipsbury pinfold, I would make
thee care for me.

OSWALD
Why dost thou use me thus? I know thee not.

KENT
Fellow, I know thee.

OSWALD
What dost thou know me for?

KENT
A knave, a rascal, an eater of broken meats; a
base, proud, shallow, beggarly, three-suited, hundred-pound,
filthy worsted-stocking knave; a lily-livered,
action-taking, whoreson, glass-gazing, superserviceable,
finical rogue; one-trunk-inheriting
slave; one that wouldst be a bawd in way of good
service, and art nothing but the composition of a
knave, beggar, coward, pander, and the son and heir

of a mongrel bitch; one whom I will beat into
clamorous whining if thou deny'st the least syllable
of thy addition.

(*KL* 2.2.7-24)

Oswald follows his mistress's idea that language is but an instrument of the weak, and he lacks the force to back up his words with any actions. He is the ultimate example in the play of "All hat, no cattle," or, "An empty suit"—i.e., there's nothing real or human, backing up his words or seemingly gentlemanly clothing, as he is only his clothes: "You cowardly rascal, nature disclaims in thee; a/tailor made thee" (*King Lear* 2.2.55-56).[7] Best for such a one to talk or bluff his way out of any messy situations. (Though cf. later, when Edgar's feigned accent, "Chill not let go, zir, without vurther 'casion" [*King Lear* 4.6.264], misleads Oswald into underestimating the skilled violence the disguised nobleman can bring to bear, and Oswald jumps into action rather too quickly for his own good.)[8] Kent, on the other hand, regards one as but prelude to the other: he talks about how savagely he'll beat Oswald, and then he does so. (Cf. above on Cordelia, who puts it in the opposite order, saying she only speaks after she has acted: "since what I well intend/I'll do 't before I speak" [*King Lear* 1.1.259-261].) And both talking about it and doing it are hugely satisfying to both Kent and the audience. Again, Kent sees words as expressing intent, and made real by actions. The only problem with language is when any of those connections (between intent, word, and deed) are broken, which is part of the implacable hatred Kent has for Oswald:

KENT
That such a slave as this should wear a sword,
Who wears no honesty. Such smiling rogues as these,
Like rats, oft bite the holy cords atwain
Which are too intrinse t' unloose; smooth every passion
That in the natures of their lords rebel.

(*KL* 2.2.74-80)

As we saw in the last chapter, Kent suffers because for him, loving Lear means loving truth, even when Lear is mad and finds the truth (and therefore Kent) abhorrent. Oswald loves neither Goneril nor the truth, and does great harm to both, ultimately (and himself).

In his exchange with the violent, evil Cornwall, Kent's candor again provokes the higher-ranking male, as it did Lear. But Cornwall's complaint against the disguised Kent is also different:

CORNWALL
This is some fellow
Who, having been praised for bluntness, doth affect
A saucy roughness and constrains the garb
Quite from his nature. He cannot flatter, he.
An honest mind and plain, he must speak truth!
An they will take it, so; if not, he's plain.
These kind of knaves I know, which in this plainness
Harbor more craft and more corrupter ends
Than twenty silly-ducking observants
That stretch their duties nicely.

KENT
Sir, in good faith, in sincere verity,
Under th' allowance of your great aspect,
Whose influence, like the wreath of radiant fire
On flick'ring Phoebus' front—

CORNWALL
What mean'st by this?

KENT
To go out of my dialect, which you discommend
so much. I know, sir, I am no flatterer. He that
beguiled you in a plain accent was a plain knave,
which for my part I will not be, though I should
win your displeasure to entreat me to 't.

(*KL* 2.2.100-120)

In a way, Cornwall sees through Kent's disguise, more than others do. He can tell Kent is putting on an act: he "doth affect," and is practicing some "craft" against them. Cornwall is only wrong as to which part is the act, which part is real, for he assumes that the "roughness" and "plainness" of Kent are part of the fakery, and underneath lies "more corrupter ends," when of course, Kent's "ends" and his bluntness are all truly him, even though he is not really a man named Caius who just happened to wander by and join up with the powerless, out-of-favor king. Again, Kent seems to carefully use language (and disguise) to present himself accurately and truthfully.

And what of Lear? We have one speech of his late in the opening scene, when he says something about his own practice of speech:

LEAR
Hear me, recreant! On thine allegiance, hear me!
That thou hast sought to make us break our vows—
Which we durst never yet—and with strained pride
To come betwixt our sentence and our power,
Which nor our nature nor our place can bear.

(*KL* 1.1.191-195)

For himself, at least, Lear believes in having his speech and actions completely coincide—nothing is to come between "our sentence and our power." Words are "vows" and Lear claims "never" to have broken any. Everything about him—his "nature" and his "place"—forbids any divergence between word and deed. And if we take "nature" and "place" as broadly as possible, I think this is an incredible claim of how Lear feels all his being—as man, father, Briton, king—relies on and forms such an integral whole.[9] Of course, given how unwise Lear shows himself in this scene, we needn't trust his claim, but as I think about the play, the claim seems accurate. His faults are about trying to dominate others, and a terrible neediness in himself, but insincerity and hypocrisy would not seem to be part of his faulty makeup. It leaves one wondering, however, along with Lear, how in the world Goneril and Regan became such committed liars and vow breakers. If not from imitation of their father, perhaps simply to avoid his (totally sincere, but not for that any more tolerable) explosions of wrath.[10] It does make the family resemblance between Lear and Cordelia striking, even if their theory of language is incompatible. "You can't make me talk, boomer!" and "You can't make me go back on my word, whipper-snapper!" are comically different in generational idiom, but frighteningly identical in their stubborn insistence on one's own integrity, or what Bloom calls Lear's "wholeheartedness."[11]

But whatever he may expect of himself, or have instilled in Cordelia, or sense in a loyal friend like Kent, Lear is shrewd enough to know many others see little connection between words and deeds. I emphasize again: he brushes aside the lying hyperbole of Goneril and Regan, fully aware they are saying what they feel is necessary (and what he has forced them into, if he were taking more responsibility), and it bears no connection to their feelings. Interestingly, Lear explicitly shows developing awareness of a kind of "language" that deliberately, by design, does not convey the thoughts of the one "speaking" it, but a set meaning, that the "speaker" adopts by using this language: this is the nonverbal communication through clothing or fashion.[12] Lear notes this succinctly when addressing Regan: "Thou art a lady;/If only to go warm were gorgeous,/Why, nature needs not what thou gorgeous wear'st,/Which scarcely keeps thee warm" (*King Lear* 2.4.307-310). The clothes Regan wears send the message or maintain the image of "lady," and have nothing to do with protection from the elements, or with what she's feeling or thinking at the moment, since she must maintain this appearance and this status all the time. This comes up repeatedly as Lear divests himself of all outer trappings (that show he is a king, an elderly father, a man): "Alack,/bareheaded?" ... "Come, unbutton here." [*Tearing off his clothes*] .... "Pull off my boots. Harder, harder. So." ... "Off, off, you lendings!/Pray you undo this button. Thank you, sir" (*King Lear* 3.2.64-65; 3.4.115-116; 4.6.191; 5.3.373),[13] representing outwardly an inner realization of the faultiness and falseness he had engaged in or bought into, when he wore such trappings.[14] We will return to this in our next chapter, because it is a part of the whole discussion of "nature" but for now, we note that Lear has a subtle and complex appreciation of language, and distinguishes several kinds, on a continuum of sincerity: for him, vows must be completely sincere and reflect inner feeling and commitment; at the other extreme, clothes are completely conventional and have no personal or inner meaning, but only the outward meaning agreed upon by society.

So Lear can hear Goneril's and Regan's pretty words, the way he can see their pretty clothes: they convey propriety, decorum, and absolutely nothing as personal as what the wearer or speaker means or values or loves—and certainly nothing as sincere as what he craves. (And has anyone ever put on the play, with Cordelia as dressed up as Goneril and Regan—whether they are provocatively or luxuriously so?[15] It would be a bold choice if they did but also simply nonsensical.) They fulfill the obligation he has imposed on them. But when he turns to Cordelia, of course, he expects the real deal, which is to say, real words communicating real feelings. He did not expect and could not accept, a third statement fulfilling obligations, but that is exactly how Cordelia phrased her answer (even after the confrontational, accusatory "Nothing"): "I love your Majesty/According to my bond, no more nor less" (*King Lear* 1.1.101-102). He expected a certain kind of resemblance between himself and his favorite child, that she would share his belief that words are hugely important, maybe even sacred. Instead he found out she was every bit his child and equal in stubbornness, and maybe even shared a bit of his insistence that love is asserting power over someone.[16] (The totally unnecessary "no more nor less" seems deliberately assertive and pointed.) That is (from her point of view) how he tried to express his love for her, by making her submit and making her beholden to him, and she did not just say, "Don't do that!" but vividly showed, "Your plan dashes itself to pieces, on the rock of my will. I am the one with power."[17] He assumed they thought alike, when in fact they felt and willed alike.

Let us elaborate on this assumed commonality of thinking about language, before we turn to Augustine. Lear has made a visual if not verbal statement to Cordelia, with the map. He has laid before her what he felt, as king or father, he was supposed to, in order to show love. If the idiom was maps and treaties and contracts, that was part of his "place" as king; if he had been a baker or bricklayer, it would have been something else, but it still would have been a concrete expression of love, if Lear was still Lear in some other "place."[18] That he demanded a particular statement from Cordelia, on command, at a specified time, in front of dozens of people—all that is monstrous bullying and neediness. But he is trying to "speak" to her, in his own "wholehearted" way, because he believes language, inner feelings, and outer actions can and should be connected and reinforce each other. If it is a hideous kind of violence and disrespect to demand, "Tell me you love me!" it is stunted and wrong in a very different way, to think, "S/he knows how I feel. I've shown it enough. I don't need to say it. It would be cheapening the love, to try to put it into words." It is wrong to demand someone say how she feels, but it's also wrong to assume someone knows how you feel. The first error is one of abusing power in the name of love, of overstepping one's bounds and limiting the other's rights and freedom; the latter is more an error of underestimating human limitations, of thinking others are nearly capable of clairvoyance or of superhuman self-sufficiency and need no reassurance, when of course all of us, many less pathological than Lear, need lots of assurance about a great many things.

For someone who left us more words than any other author from antiquity, it is ironic indeed that Augustine is in some ways, at some times, very close to agreeing with Cordelia's idea of language (that the best, most important things in life do not admit of being put into words, at least not the "regular" words we all form and encounter), with a dose of Kent's feeling (that blunt, simple language is best, and all elevated language is to be regarded with suspicion). Augustine begins theorizing about language in *Confessions* as soon as he has described what he believes is the self-evident, constantly observed state of children:

> The only innocent feature in babies is the weakness of their frames; the minds of infants are far from innocent. I have watched and experienced for myself the jealousy of a small child: he could not even speak, yet he glared with livid fury at his fellow nursling. Everyone has seen this. (*Conf.* 1.7.11)

If the infant "mind" is sinful, then to teach children language is just to give them another, more refined, precise way to express their sinful thoughts, feelings, and intentions. The inarticulate scream and the silent glare give way to increasingly better formulated insults, mockery, demands, hate- and need-filled speech of all kinds. Just as adult bodies are more dangerous than infant ones (only because larger and stronger), so adult minds are better equipped to harm and deceive. They are not lessened in their sinfulness, however. And language is an important part of that adult arsenal:

> In this way I gradually built up a collection of words, observing them as they were used in their proper places in different sentences and hearing them frequently. I came to understand which things they signified, and by schooling my own mouth to utter them I declared my wishes by using the same signs. Thus I learned to express my needs to the people among whom I lived, and they made their wishes known to me; and I waded deeper

> into the stormy world of human life, although I was still subject to the authority of my parents and the guidance of my elders. (*Conf.* 1.8.13)

Language just pushes young Augustine "deeper into the stormy world of human life." It is not even a loss of innocence (because neither he nor anyone else ever had innocence to lose), but a journey deeper into the darkness and storm of adult life. How interesting and revealing of their two visions, almost inverted on this point, that Augustine puts the storm right at the beginning of one's life, and as a constitutive element of everyone diving deeper into sin, while Shakespeare reserves it for the end of Lear's life (though the middle of the play), and makes of it a corrective, educational stripping away of his sinful habits.

Augustine sees the sinfulness in language immediately in the kind of language he prefers as a young boy, and the kind in which his society prefers to marinate him:

> Latin studies, on the contrary, I loved, not the elementary kind under my first teachers, but the lessons taught by masters of literature; for the early lessons in reading, writing and arithmetic had been no less burdensome and boring to me than all the elements of Greek. What other reason could there be for this than the sinful, inane pride in my life, flesh as I was, a passing breath that comes not again? Those early lessons in literacy were unquestionably more profitable because more dependable; by means of them I was gradually being given a power which became mine and still remains with me: the power to read any piece of writing I come across and to write anything I have a mind to myself. Far more useful, then, were those studies than others in which I was forced to memorize the wanderings of some fellow named Aeneas, while forgetting my own waywardness, and to weep over Dido, who killed herself for love, when all the while in my intense misery I put up with myself with never a tear, as I died away from you, O God, who are my life. (*Conf.* 1.13.20)

Interesting here, that the ability to read and write (and before that, speak and listen), are at least "profitable" and "dependable" (if still prone to sin). But in the content of what young Augustine (and all the other boys of his social class) was forced to read and write (and then grew to love reading about!), he saw a further manifestation of the sinfulness we saw in our previous chapter—the sinfulness of loving love, rather than loving (a real, appropriate object or person). But here it is taken even a further step removed: after all, one can't say one loves Dido, or even loves loving her, because one has never been properly introduced to the queen of ancient Carthage. Augustine describes falling in love with reading about her loving, becoming obsessed with and enthralled by the linguistic and emotional rollercoaster of *The Aeneid*, rather than enjoying (and working to improve) the real ride of one's own life. And such odd fascination with unreality only becomes more addictive when on stage, rather than on the page:

> I was held spellbound by theatrical shows full of images that mirrored by own wretched plight and further fueled the fire within me. Why is it one likes being moved to grief at the sight of sad or tragic events on stage, when one would be unwilling to suffer the same things oneself? In the capacity of spectator one welcomes sad feelings; in fact, the sadness itself is the pleasure. What incredible stupidity! (*Conf.* 3.2.2)

We have moved further on in falsity even than sentimentality (loving love), into voyeurism (loving beholding a depiction of someone else's love), sometimes even of a particularly perverse, nonsensical kind of voyeurism that blends into curiosity in the bad sense (loving beholding the depiction of someone else's pain or misery or death).

Augustine describes this even going beyond his reading habits, into his writing and speaking, because he is being trained to produce and perform such literature himself, as an exercise, as he learns to speak more persuasively:[19]

> An exercise was set for me which was fraught with worrying implications, for I hoped to win praise and honor if I succeeded, but if not, I ran the risk of being caned. I was required to produce a speech made by Juno expressing her anger and grief at being unable to repulse the Trojan king from Italy, but in words which I had never heard Juno use. We were obliged to follow the errant footsteps of poetic fantasies and to express in prose what the poet had said in verse. That boy was adjudged the best speaker who most convincingly suggested emotions

> of anger and grief and clothed them in apt words, as befitted the dignity of the person represented. What did it profit me, O God, my true life, that my speech was acclaimed above those of my many peers and fellow-students? Was it not all smoke and wind? Was there no other material on which I could have exercised my intelligence and my tongue? Yes, there was: your praise, O Lord; your praise in the words of the scriptures would have supported the drooping vine of my soul, and then it would not have yielded a crop of worthless fruit for the birds to carry off. (*Conf.* 1.17.27)

Exactly as with what they read, the boys' writing and speaking are false and misleading— "errant ... fantasies .... smoke and wind ... worthless." And here we have a worse, more sinful motive introduced—love of being praised oneself. Now language (according to Augustine) is revealed not just as deceptive and misleading, but its speakers are growing proud at how deceptive they have learned to be, showing it off, being rewarded and praised for it, and thereby wanting to do it more, as they grow more adept at the deception. By the end of that paragraph, Augustine is sadly confessing of having sought praise for himself, rather than praising God. The love of praise is sinful enough, but devoting oneself to it when one could be praising God, is that much worse, pointless, and debased.

Before moving on in Augustine's evolving indictment of language, we should pause to consider a question rather obviously implied by the present work: How can one even connect Augustine and Shakespeare, when Augustine was such a notorious critic of imaginative, fictional literature in general, and the theater, specifically? Honestly, when I first thought of pairing Augustine and Shakespeare in this book, I really mostly thought of the irony, almost naughtiness of it. How counterintuitive—maybe even transgressive?—to make an illustration or embodiment of Augustine's thought, out of one of the greatest masterpieces of imaginative literature, when Augustine rails so passionately and repeatedly against the epic and dramatic literature of his own education? How potentially transgressive also, in the other direction, to make a play that is often thought of as purely secular and nihilistic,[20] into a Trojan horse full of little Augustines ready to jump out and scold us into submission to their dark, "god-haunted," but weirdly uplifting (to me) vision of reality.[21] But really, my instinct to pair the two works may not be as contrary to Augustine's views as would seem at first, or as I thought when I started. Would Augustine be able to see the positive value of imaginative literature? As a matter of personal preference, and given how negatively he experienced it in his own life, I have to suspect not, if I'm being honest. But can we defend imaginative literature, like *King Lear*, from some or all of the accusations and criticisms Augustine levels against it? I think at least partly. Am I in love with the pain I see on stage when I watch the play? Of course. For a couple hours the immediate experience is overwhelming (if done right), and sweeps me up in some unthinking, passive (if exhilarating) experience of feeling (cf. above on wrestling). But the ability—I would almost say necessity—of stepping back after and analyzing the play, and my feelings, I think takes us to a place of awareness, introspection, and analysis, that looks rather like what Augustine engages in with *Confessions*. If for a moment, I'm loving just pain, then for days and years after, I'm considering what to do and how to feel and what to think, in light of that experience.[22] I am also, whatever the theory, very intensely experiencing beauty, both in the moment in the theater and in the later reflection on the experience, and such intense immersion in beauty is probably worth some risk, given the edifying possibilities Augustine sees in beauty.[23] And as for Augustine's self-accusation that he loved being praised more than praising God: Do I love being praised for my analysis of *King Lear*? Again—of course. But no more so than I love being praised as an Augustine scholar. (I said I never called myself that, but I'm also honest enough to admit I rather like it when other people use that title to refer to me.) That really seems like an accusation that could be made against any human endeavor in which one might excel and take pride (scholarship, musical talent, athleticism, etc.).

Augustine continues his critique of language, considering his own career for which his education was preparing him. He observes in his elders, and mimics in his own behavior, the pride and love of praise he had already observed:

> Such were the moral standards of the world at whose threshold I lay, a wretched boy; this was the arena in which I was to struggle. It made me more wary of committing some barbarism in speech than of being jealous of others who did not commit it when I did. I tell you this, my God, and confess to you those efforts for

> which I was praised; for at that time I believed that living a good life consisted in winning the favor of those who commended me. (*Conf.* 1.19.30)

If anything, the qualities for which praise is being sought, and mockery being avoided, are even more paltry than in his previous example, for Augustine considers how he did not just pursue skill in writing and speaking vividly and descriptively, but how he grew fearful of committing minor grammatical mistakes, and fell into the sin of envy of those who successfully avoided such.

But the "persistent search of fame" doesn't end with just overly fastidious observance of grammatical rules:

> A man in persistent search of fame pleads before a merely human judge, with a crowd of other humans standing round, and accuses his adversary with savage hatred. He takes the utmost care that no slip of the tongue betrays him into saying, "them fellows ...," while caring not a whit that by his rage he is about to remove a fellow-human from human society. (*Conf.* 1.18.29)

Here Augustine considers again the motives behind speech, and the results from it, and not just its outward forms. And as usual, the intent and consequences are far worse than the pettiness of seeking praise in trivial matters. It includes using words to do actual (physical) harm to others. "Sticks and stones may break my bones, but names can never hurt me": we all knew that to be untrue in elementary school, when words hurt us deeply (or when we witnessed the pain we could cause others with our words). Then how much more so in the court or senate, wielded by much better trained and practiced persons, people much more intelligent and powerful than children, but just as sinful? All this together—the seeking after praise, the obsession with beautiful but untrue speech, the focus on trivial matters of style rather than substance and meaning, and the abuse of language to result in real oppression and domination—leads Augustine to see his career as a teacher of rhetoric, as incompatible with his newfound life and belief as a Christian:

> I believed it to be pleasing in your sight that I should withdraw the service of my tongue from the market of speechifying, so that

> young boys who were devoting their thoughts not to your law, not to your peace, but to lying follies and legal battles, should no longer buy from my mouth the weapons for their frenzy. (*Conf.* 9.2.2)

His continuation of his career seems almost more threatening to his spiritual well-being than his more vividly (hyperbolically) described avoidance of chastity, as it threatened to cause real harm and continue a sinful lifestyle and society, on into the next generation (and beyond). Also, although "concubinage" (having a baby mama) was considered acceptable, it was not admired,[24] as was a professorship, and an admired sinful behavior is surely more dangerous, long term, than one that is furtively pursued, as there are even more reasons not to give it up. But whatever their relative urgency, the two renunciations (career and sex) are presented by Augustine as both necessary for his new life in Christ.[25]

But the particular bad habits of "the market of speechifying" (and what a biting self-criticism, to give such a mocking label to one's career in which one had invested years) do not end with arrogant preening over the right use of pronouns (or scornful mocking of those who don't), or the indulging in hyperbole to create pretty descriptions of unreal things. They extend even to causing avoidance of the truth, because it is cloaked in humble, simple language and does not reach the heights of rhetorical flourish that other expressions do:[26]

> Accordingly I turned my attention to the holy scriptures to find out what they were like. What I see in them today is something not accessible to the scrutiny of the proud nor exposed to the gaze of the immature, something lowly as one enters but lofty as one advances further, something veiled in mystery. At that time, though, I was in no state to enter, nor prepared to bow my head and accommodate myself to its ways. My approach then was quite different than the one I'm suggesting now: when I studied the Bible and compared it with Cicero's dignified prose, it seemed to me unworthy. My swollen pride recoiled from its style and my intelligence failed to penetrate to its inner meaning. Scripture is a reality that grows along with little children, but I disdained to be a little child and in my high and mighty arrogance regarded myself as grown up. (*Conf.* 3.5.9)

If sinful desire for goods (and also that others not have them, as well as grasping at them oneself), that Augustine claims to see even in infants before they are capable of speech, is the earliest, most primal manifestation and urge of original sin, by the time one is in adolescence and beyond, many of us have moved on to "swollen pride" as the more usual expression of our sinful nature. And as with other elements that Augustine critiques about human speech, it is the falsifying that most shames him as he considers himself years later. If beautiful language was more persuasive, and crude language less so, that might be a tolerable (and somewhat understandable) situation for human speech. We might be guilty of a certain aesthetic preciosity in language, but as long as we did not ignore simply put speech, we could still pursue truth. But Augustine comes to believe, much like Kent, that simple, blunt language is in fact the best conveyor of truth, because it shows the speaker and listener to be humble, in every sense of the word. But for those thoroughly invested and practiced in deception hidden by pretty words, simple language is repulsive, because it insults their pride, and threatens to expose their real, untruthful values.

By the time Augustine encounters the rival teachers of Faustus (for the Manichees), and Ambrose (for Catholic orthodoxy), he is beginning partly to overcome these prejudices. This is clearest with Faustus, whose "pleasant and smooth" delivery leaves Augustine unimpressed:

> When he came, then, he did indeed impress me as a man of pleasant and smooth speech, who chattered on the usual themes much more beguilingly than the rest. A man adept at serving finer wines, then; but what was that to me in my thirst? My ears were sated with such offerings already. The content did not seem better to me for being better presented, nor true because skillfully expressed, nor the man wise of soul because he had a handsome face and a graceful turn of speech. Those who had held out promises to me were not good judges; to them he seemed wise and prudent merely because they enjoyed the way he talked. But I realized that there were people of a different stamp who doubted even the possibility of truth, and were unwilling to trust anything conveyed in elegant and fluent style. (*Conf.* 5.6.10)

Augustine has been "sated" with such speech; now he longs for "content." But if one gets too suspicious and distrustful of speech, one swings to the opposite extreme of skepticism, and doubts "even the possibility of truth." By the time he writes *Confessions*, Augustine believes he should have been learning to accept the truthfulness of simple language, but instead he became for a time "unwilling to trust anything conveyed in elegant and fluent style." Instead of trusting the right words (and ideas), Augustine despairs of any connection between truth and language (like Cordelia), or even the existence of truth itself (going far further than Cordelia).

Ambrose is a more fascinating but confusing case for Augustine—a polished speaker who tells the truth (as Augustine believes it when he is writing).[27] Not the glib but specious and lightweight Faustus, not the coarse, homespun (and seemingly too literal) truths of the Bible, Ambrose presents himself something like a Christian Cicero (all of this seeking for wisdom and truth having begun years before for Augustine, when he read Cicero's *Hortensius* [*Conf.* 3.4.7])[28] — learned, eloquent, subtle, steeped in both classical (even including Greek)[29] and biblical thought:

> With professional interest I listened to him conducting disputes before the people, but my intention was not the right one: I was assessing his eloquence to see whether it matched its reputation. I wished to ascertain whether the readiness of speech with which rumor credited him was really there, or something more, or less. I hung keenly upon his words, but cared little for their content, and indeed despised it, as I stood there delighting in the sweetness of his discourse. Though more learned than that of Faustus it was less light-hearted and beguiling; but such criticism concerns the style only, for with regard to the content there was no comparison. (*Conf.* 5.13.23)

Augustine is still immersed in the world, values, and aesthetics of rhetoric, and so he still notes, and is somewhat held back, by perceived stylistic deficiencies in Ambrose's sermons. But even so, he "hung keenly upon his words," and the "content" was making an impression that Faustus never could. Augustine's account of Faustus is one of bitter and complete disappointment, ending almost with despair that truth could ever be found—maybe that it didn't even exist. Augustine's account of Ambrose is more of a man bemused, and confounded by how and from whom he hears new, challenging ideas in attractive, elevated, and still somehow familiar, language.[30]

As noted, the encounter with Faustus was so disorienting, and the speeches of Ambrose hopeful but still not definitive enough, that Augustine then took a detour into skepticism (*Conf.* 5.14.25). But not just the specific ideas of Ambrose lingered, but his method of seeking truth in many texts and traditions,[31] of joyfully finding surprising unity and agreement, between and among the most unexpected passages. I think this is the best way to explain Augustine's juxtaposing and claiming agreement between such disparate texts, as he approaches his final steps toward accepting Christian belief and life:

> You wanted to show me first and foremost how you thwart the proud but give grace to the humble, and with what immense mercy on your part the way of humility was demonstrated to us when your Word was made flesh and dwelt among men and women; and so through a certain man grossly swollen with pride you provided me with some books by the Platonists, translated from the Greek into Latin. In them I read (not that the same words were used, but precisely the same doctrine was taught, buttressed by many and various arguments) that *in the beginning was the Word, and the Word was with God; he was God. He was with God in the beginning. Everything was made through him; nothing came to be without him. What was made is alive with his life, and that life was the light of humankind. The Light shines in the darkness, and the darkness has never been able to master it.* (*Conf.* 7.9.13; Jn 1:1-4)

This is the unity of all truth, that I think every good teacher tries to coax their students to see, whatever the subject being studied.[32] It doesn't matter if the fourth evangelist never read "some books by the Platonists." It does not matter if the Platonists were pre- or non- or even anti-Christian in their beliefs. When people find the truth (and contra the skeptics, there is truth and it is findable), and they express it, even if not in "the same words," then their words are communicating the same truth (because there is only one truth).[33] Despite all the sinful infections that have warped it historically or in his own life, Augustine has finally arrived at an experience of language and truth, like Lear longed for—that language can convey truth, that truth is containable in human speech.

But what so enraged Lear, and so long confused Augustine, is the allusive, mysterious, non-propositional character of some (and maybe the best) language, and the experiential dimension of truth that transcends language. Lear didn't really know *what* he wanted to hear from Cordelia: none of us do, from our beloved, because the beloved has to have some element of mystery and danger about her. But we emphatically know when we don't hear it. And Augustine couldn't just read the gospel, or hear Ambrose, or read or hear anyone or anything else, and get the experience he wanted (needed) of God: truths about God are communicable in speech, but God is not. (If God were, we would be stuck with some kind if stunted bibliolatry, and perhaps some of us long for that simpler dogma.) For that, full and humble and personal presence, rather than objective, detached, propositional language, is necessary: "but that *the Word was made flesh and dwelt among us*, I did not read there" (*Conf.* 7.9.14; Jn 1:14).

And that is why at the climactic moment of Augustine's "conversion" it is again words—words telling him to read other words!—that move him. But they are not "regular" words, not a sermon or essay or even scripture:

> I went on talking like this and weeping in the intense bitterness of my broken heart. Suddenly I heard a voice from a house nearby—perhaps a voice of some boy or girl, I do not know—singing over and over again, "Pick it up and read, pick it up and read." (*Conf.* 8.12.29)

The whole scene is almost hallucinatory or dream-like—"perhaps" this happened, "I do not know," and he goes on to wonder about any logical explanation for such a chant (e.g., a children's game that involves such singing) but can think of none. And even when he turns to the very apt biblical passage (Rom. 13:13-14)—well, so what? He had been convinced of the rightness of this course of action for some time. The passage had been in the Bible the whole time, along with many other salutary pieces of advice, and many other rather less appropriate lines. And the method of picking passages at random had been specifically (and to my mind, very appropriately) mocked and discounted by Augustine earlier in *Confessions*:

> Think how frequently it happens, he said, that a person looks for guidance in the pages of some poet who was singing of an unrelated matter and had something quite different in mind, yet a line stands out which is wonderfully apposite to the question in hand, well, then, surely we should not wonder if, in response to some prompting from above, an utterance issues from a human mind unaware of what is happening in it, and this utterance corresponds to the circumstances and actions of the client. This would be chance, not skill. (*Conf.* 4.3.5)

I have no doubt Augustine thinks God spoke to him that day—I am not being cynical about the episode specifically, or *Confessions* more generally.[34] My only point here is that a bunch of words worked as a call from God that had not worked that way the day before, or on other people, or at other places. When I checked the reference just now, typing this paragraph, I got no special feeling or meaning from Romans 13:13-14. If above we saw Augustine conclude that many different words (whether from John the Evangelist or Plotinus, Latin or Greek) can convey the same truth, here we see the same words might be full of truth at one time to one person, and completely insignificant, to that person or others, at other times.

After all this analysis of language, let us return to *King Lear* for two final cautionary or qualifying statements on the subject. Both are (probably significantly) from Edgar, the character who learns and changes and grows the most in the play.[35] In disguise as a mad beggar, Poor Tom, Edgar is considering the wheel of fortune,[36] that represents one's life as it cycles through good and bad and back to good. He opines, in the abstract, that it's better to be in the bad part of the cycle, because then things will get better (whereas being in the good part of the cycle brings fear and anxiety that the good times will end). But then he is confronted with his newly blinded father, helpless, covered in blood, and the theoretical musings seem somewhat less helpful, as he wants desperately for this pain to be alleviated immediately, not in due course. But then he considers further, that one (for better or worse) doesn't know how big the wheel is, and hence one cannot tell if there's more bad into which one is descending, or if one has reached the nadir. But as part of that, Edgar also claims something about saying such an evaluation: "And worse I may be yet. The worst is not/So long as we can say 'This is the worst'" (*King Lear* 4.1.30-31). There is something going on here about the human capacity to put things into words, and thereby have some control over them. So if I am suffering and I say I am, or say it's the worst, I have the consolation that I have not yet lost the ability to speak or make that measurement. Job's suffering is human suffering precisely because he can complain of it, and so is Edgar's. So is his father's, who can still speak, and who says his loss of sight is rather an improvement for him (*King Lear* 4.1.19-25). All of this is to say, that though we have found nuances for speech in these two masterpieces, speech itself is a brute fact, a given of human existence. It has implications and results, it can be studied and dissected, done better or worse, but silence is not an option. On this point, perhaps Cordelia's is the most wrong of all the views we have examined: her idea of the inadequacy of language would almost make of it something we can outgrow or rise above, and that simply is untrue to our human nature (I almost daresay, essence).

The play concludes with Edgar's plea for the right use of language: "The weight of this sad time we must obey,/Speak what we feel, not what we ought to say" (*King Lear* 5.3.392-393). On a stage covered with corpses, it is a staggering evaluation that insincerity and false speech are what brought down all this horror on them. But whose? Goneril and Regan are easy enough to condemn with this or practically any other criteria of human decency: they did not speak what they felt, they only said what they thought they were supposed to. But how this evaluation would apply to Cordelia I think is harder to say, more mysterious. She definitely didn't say what she was supposed to. But did she say what she felt? Further analysis of her response still awaits us in Chapter 4, but I think I will say for now—yes and no. She did not say her love—she simply denied the possibility of saying it, and denied the legitimacy of asking for the statement. Both are true enough, as I've said above, but again miss something of the frailty of people, of young women and daughters, of old men and fathers.

I feel as though one really cannot conclude a chapter on the problem of language without reference to the classic scene from *Dead Poets Society* (1989), because its searing, painful truthfulness comes from the same places as what we have been examining in Shakespeare and Augustine—from a head and heart considering each other carefully and honestly, and trying to connect with other heads and hearts. The teacher, John Keating (played by Robin Williams in the way where he was at his best, by being manic and explosive, but with moments of restraint and calm and focus), asks his students (all boys), "What is the purpose of language?" They are mostly confused—stunned into silence, really—because their education until then has always been on the *how* of everything (e.g., how to spell, how to add, how to diagram a sentence, etc.), but never on the *why* (e.g., why speak or write at all?). One volunteers the bland definition of "To communicate." Keating shoots back, "No! To woo women." Allowing for a gender specificity that was already kind of quaint verging on the out of touch when the film was released, the quotation takes us back to exactly what we have examined in *King Lear* and *Confessions*. Keating is fully an idealist when it comes to language, and that is what he is trying to impress on his young charges—that language is so precious because it is how one conducts something as important and personal as getting someone else to know one loves him or her, and to elicit the same kinds of feelings in return (also expressed in language?). If anything, Keating is close to Lear's wish and Augustine's climactic experience that language *can be* a reflection or projection of some inner reality, not just a distortion or obfuscation. And of course there's some of the Fool in Keating's character, always challenging, truth telling, mocking, doing outrageous things to get his students to pay attention and think.

But in the film's tragic ending, there is some honest acknowledgment of how such a view is so different from that of the rest of the world, obsessed with appearances or career or propriety, and how ultimately that unidealistic world cannot be wished away or ignored or cajoled into changing its ways to allow for idealists. If language can be how Keating or Lear imagines it is, it must also be frankly admitted, it is most often how Goneril and Regan and Edmund proudly and loudly use it throughout the play, and how Augustine shamefully looks back on it in his early career: a useful mask to make dealing with unpleasant people go as smoothly as possible, to exercise power over others when possible (and when physical force isn't advisable), and something not ever to be mistaken as having any connection to what (if anything) goes on behind the mask. The hope that we can ever live a life where we "Speak what we feel, not what we ought to say" (*King Lear* 5.3.393) seems very unlikely to ever be fulfilled in the world of *King Lear*. Though to be fair and more optimistic: if it ever could be, it would be by someone as painfully, thoroughly schooled in language and love and actions, as Edgar has been in the course of the play. On Augustine's side, I leave it up to the reader's imagination, how much the busy life of a bishop—forced to deal with so many parishioners, fellow bishops and clergy, various "heretics" and schismatics, as well as the secular government, all while successive waves of barbarians threatened—could instantiate this ideal of language, feeling, and truth working and flowing together, without the disappointing compromises and rhetorical manipulations typical of a political life. I personally would think such loving, truthful discourse was only really and fully a part of Augustine's own life very briefly at Cassiciacum, though I am sure, for someone as gregarious and loquacious as he, hoping for an eternal life filled with joyful, truthful speech, would be exactly how he would imagine blessedness and communion with others and with God.

Notes

1 Cf. Williams, *Tragic Imagination*, 39, who describes more of the dynamic that is set up between the responses of Goneril and Cordelia: "What he does not expect is that it should turn out to be literally inexpressible. Goneril—as A. D. Nuttall notes in his brief and penetrating discussion of the play—begins with the 'inexpressibility topos' ('I love you more than words can wield the matter')—which means that Cordelia cannot even say what she can't say: it's as if the currency of inarticulacy as well as of articulacy has been debased by Goneril's theatrical foreclosure." More briefly, that although Lear thought to advantage Cordelia by having her speak last, it disadvantages her by forcing her into a kind of "Me-too-ism" in her speech (which she emphatically rejects, but that then also disappoints her father).

2 On the importance of language, see Edelstein, *Thinking Shakespeare*, 13: "Thought needs language to come into the world. A dramatic character *needs* the words he says, because without them his thoughts wouldn't exist in the world outside himself. His intention to communicate, his desire to effect some change in the reality around him—these are the engines that drive thought from deep inside a character's mind all the way to another's ear, and then out across the footlights and up to the back row of the balcony" (emphasis in original).

3 Cf. Booth, "Greatness of *King Lear*," 67: "We exult with her but we may well be put off by the cold competence .... Cordelia is justified in all that she says, but not lovable." Also Rice, "Empathic Edgar," 51: "Cordelia is more concerned with the spiritual pride of her integrity, at the beginning, and the rightness of her position *vis a vis* her sisters, near the end, than with love. Her self-image interferes with her ability to love." But cf. Lionel Basney, "Is a Christian Perspective on Shakespeare Productive and/or Necessary?" in *Shakespeare and the Christian Tradition*, edited by E. Beatrice Batson (Lewiston, NY: Edwin Mellen Press, 1994), 19–35, esp. 30, where he notes this may be more our problem of perception: "Part of unease with Cordelia centers on the priority in her mind of obligations as a form of love. We assume—it is part of the insanity of our cultural morality—that love and obligation are opposites."

4 Cf. Basney, "Is a Christian Perspective on Shakespeare Productive and/or Necessary?" 30: "Yet the exclamatory language, the language of explicit feeling, has been monopolized by Goneril and Regan. It has become simple a discourse of exchange: say this and get this."

5 Cf. John L. Murphy, *Darkness and Devils: Exorcism and King Lear* (Athens, OH, and London: Ohio University Press, 1984), 177–8: "The controlling intent of the lines is, as I take them, that Kent has to mimic the manners and sentiment of a plain-bluff-Protestant-English serving man, soldier or personal attendant .... they [Kent, the Fool, Edgar] seek to bring about an intellectual and imaginative awakening on the part of the old king and the old earl to the folly of simple acquiescence in or simple opposition to the domination of their minds and spirits by this pious charade masking a Machiavellian policy of ambition and appetite."

6 Some of Edgar's speeches to his father are similarly lying but truthful. See Phyllis Rackin, "On Edgar: Delusion as Resolution," in *Twentieth Century Interpretations of King Lear: A Collection of Critical Essays,* edited by Janet Adelman (Englewood Cliffs, NJ: Prentice-Hall, 1978), 123–5, esp. 124: "What Edgar says, of course, is literally a lie, although symbolically perfectly true."

7 As noted by Thelma Nelson Greenfield, "The Clothing Motif in King Lear," *Shakespeare Quarterly* 5 (1954): 281–6, esp. 281. See also Rackin, "On Edgar," 124–5: "The passage takes its meaning from the symbolic association of 'clothes' in *King Lear* with the whole structure of values and practices that govern, protect, and disguise men in society. Oswald is so completely and so merely the creature of the social hierarchy that he serves as a perfect revelation of its limitations .... If the poor, bare, forked animal needs clothes to distinguish him from the beasts, the thing made by a tailor lacks

even the natural affections that distinguish the beasts from inanimate things."

8 Cf. Rackin, "On Edgar," 124: "Edgar's second trick is played on Oswald. Edgar speaks in a rustic dialect to reinforce Oswald's impression that he is a peasant .... Oswald's fault throughout has been that he is completely the creature of the social and political hierarchy, unaware of any values beyond worldly status or any code beyond manners."

9 Cf. Morris, *Shakespeare's God*, 349, who relates it to kingship: "While it is not to be doubted that personal whim plays some part in Lear's reaction to Kent's demand that he should revoke the pronouncement he has made, Lear's fury arises in the main from the challenge to royal authority, and the attempt, in making a king break his vow, to rend apart the personal and political. A king who has sworn must be firm: the consciousness and the reality of power can only be maintained if the possessor identifies himself with the ideal which confers it."

10 Cf. Bloom, *Shakespeare*, 509: "The foregrounding of this play would involve a long career of outbursts, which presumably helped convert Regan and Goneril into mincing hypocrites, and the favorite Cordelia into someone who has learned the gift of patient silence."

11 See Bloom, *Shakespeare*, 509: "Lear's rashness, at its most destructive, remains a wholeheartedness .... Cordelia, tragic heroine, requires no redemption, and Lear's enormous changes, his flashes of compassion and of social insight, essentially are emanations of his wholeheartedness." Cf. Morris, *Shakespeare's God*, 342, who refers to Lear's "pitiless integrity in self-criticism" and "greatness of spirit."

12 For historicist criticism related to *King Lear* and clothing, see Judy Kronenfeld, *King Lear and the Naked Truth: Rethinking the Language of Religion and Resistance* (Durham, NC, and London: Duke University Press, 1998). Much earlier (relating it to other Elizabethan drama), see Greenfield, "The Clothing Motif in *King Lear*."

13 See also the Quarto stage direction at 4.6.98, "Enter Lear, mad bedecked with weeds," which productions variously incorporate as some change of costume. For a good introductory discussion of the differences between Quarto and Folio generally, see Edelstein, *Thinking Shakespeare*, 155–7. On the differences in *King Lear* particularly, see M. J. Warren, "Quarto and Folio *King Lear* and the Interpretation of Albany and Edgar," in *William Shakespeare's King Lear*, edited by Harold Bloom (New York: Chelsea House, 1987), 45–56.

14 Cf. Rodney Delasanta, "Putting off the Old Man and Putting on the New: Ephesians 4:22–24 in Chaucer, Shakespeare, Swift, and Dostoevsky," *Christianity and Literature* 51 (2002): 339–62, esp. 343, noting how Lear's progressive disrobing "corresponds to a pattern of self-discovery that releases the Old Man in him, however falteringly, from clueless egoism, to heroic self-pity, to empathy for the suffering of others, to a grace-provoked, unbuttoned leap of faith, in the final seconds of his life, to transcendence itself. It is almost as if Shakespeare were presciently dramatizing Soren Kierkegaard's three stages-from the aesthetic, to the ethical, to the religious."

15 Cf. Greenfield, "Clothing Motif in *King Lear*," 281: "This costuming of Regan, Oswald, and others of their ilk made effective stage contrast with the quiet simplicity of Cordelia's gowns, the rough garments worn by Kent, the rags of poor Tom and finally the disarray of Lear himself."

16 Cf. Bloom, *Shakespeare*, 508 (more sympathetically to Cordelia): "Lear and all three daughters suffer from a plethora of prides, though Cordelia's legitimate concern is with what John Keats would have called the holiness of her heart's affections."

17 Cf. Morris, *Shakespeare's God*, 354: "Cordelia asserts, not only the slightness of her love for her father, but that the formality and power of his ideal is shallow and ridiculous. Lear is made to face the alternatives of rendering his kingship an absurdity by coming to terms with the person who has challenged it, or breaking the bond of love which links him with his child."

18 Cf. Morris, *Shakespeare's God*, 352: "The gesture that brings his authority to an end would reconcile the two main tendencies of his being: the last minutes of his reign will reward his children's love with lands and rule, and proclaim the warm affection that has for so long been hidden beneath his purple robes of state."

19 On similar rhetorical training 1,200 years later, see Edelstein, *Thinking Shakespeare*, 101: "But in Shakespeare's age, rhetoric was something else entirely. It was an art form, a noble field of study worthy of a lifetime's pursuit. In the context of Shakespeare's plays, rhetoric is, essentially, the art of using language to persuade. Rhetoric is also the study of that art. Rhetoric was at the heart of Shakespeare's education. He would have been taught all of its rules and technical devices. He would then have written compositions in which he argued one side or another of a question posed by his teacher."

20 Cf. Bloom, *Shakespeare*, 491: "Leo Tolstoy raged against *King Lear*, partly because he accurately sensed the drama's profound nihilism, but also out of creative envy, and perhaps, too, be had the uncanny premonition that Lear's scenes upon the heath would approximate his own final moments."

21 I'm playing on Flannery O'Connor's description of the South as "Christ-haunted" (from her 1960 lecture, "Some Aspects of the Grotesque in Southern Fiction," available online at http://www.en.utexas.edu/Classes/Bremen/e316k/316kprivate/scans/grotesque.html). I worry that Augustine is more "Father-" than "Christ-haunted," so I left it at "God."

22 Cf. Williams, *Tragic Imagination*, 42: "But that contemplation has a price: this is suffering about which we cannot make any difference, fixed in the narrative as we are fixed in our seats as spectators. We are made both to sense that we are not passive and to recognize that there is no action open to us except words and reflection. We cannot change the narrative for those who are involved in it. What then can we change? Presumably our own repertoire of responses to pain in ourselves or each other."

23 Thus Miles, *Augustine and the Fundamentalist's Daughter*, 41: "Both Plotinus and Augustine taught that the primary characteristic of the universe is beauty, and beauty is enough—richly, abundantly, enough. So it is my responsibility to train my eye to see the great beauty that forms and informs all living beings."

24 Cf. Peter Brown, *Augustine of Hippo: A Biography*, Forty-Fifth Anniversary Edition (Berkeley and Los Angeles: University of California Press, 2000; first published, 1967) 51: "Concubinage of this kind was a traditional feature of Roman life. Even the Catholic church was prepared to recognize it, provided that the couple remained faithful to one another .... A respectable arrangement, of course, need not be a particularly civilized one. No Late Roman gentleman, for instance, wrote poems to his concubine. She would be his housekeeper, the mother of his sons, of considerably lower class than himself."

25 Cf. James M. Farrell, "The Rhetoric(s) of St. Augustine's Confessions," *Augustinian Studies* 39 (2) (2008): 265–91, esp. 265: "As a result, Augustine's denunciation of his rhetorical past at the climax of his autobiographical account is seen as a parallel to his denial of worldly desires and pleasures of the flesh, and this is a reading Augustine encourages."

26 Cf. Vaught, *Journey toward God in Augustine's* Confessions. *Books I–VI*, 78: "By contrast, one must reverse the direction of philosophical eros and become a child again to find the hidden depths of a biblical text."

27 Cf. Vaught, *Journey toward God in Augustine's* Confessions. *Books I–VI*, 135: "Along with the eloquence he prizes, the ideas of Ambrose come into his mind; and as he listens to his sermons, he cannot separate their form from their content."

28 Cf. Paul R. Kolbet, *Augustine and the Cure of Souls* (Notre Dame, IN: University of Notre Dame Press, 2010) 92: "With none of the

reticence of Bishop Ambrose, Augustine's earliest writings extol 'philosophy' in language worthy of the *Hortensius*." Also Vaught, *Journey toward God in Augustine's* Confessions. *Books I–VI*, 75: "Yet long before he writes the *Confessions*, the first step toward being able to do this is the glimpse of truth in Cicero that transcends the rhetorical tradition. For the first time, Augustine sees beyond images to something more fundamental that will transform his life."

29 Cf. Brown, *Augustine of Hippo*, 74: "Ambrose had enjoyed all the advantages of an upper-class education in Rome itself. There was nothing 'provincial' about him. Thus, unlike Augustine, he cold read Greek fluently. He could comb the books of a brilliant new generation of Greek bishops and a whole tradition of Greek Christian scholarship, to give his congregation some of the most learned and up-to-date sermons in the Latin world. Nor did he have any scruples about borrowing from the pagans: he gloried in being able to parade his spoils from the pulpit—this 'gold of the Egyptians' was fair prize."

30 Cf. Vaught, *Journey toward God in Augustine's* Confessions. *Books I–VI*, 141: "Augustine's principal problem is how to bring the spirit of Faustus and the knowledge of Ambrose together. In more systematic terms, Augustine must learn how to unite two senses of the Word, one of which points to the act of speaking and the other of which calls our attention to the content spoken."

31 Cf. Brown, *Augustine of Hippo*, 76: "Ambrose, therefore, introduced Augustine to some totally new ideas .... Augustine may have arrived gradually at these ideas, and it is exceptionally difficult to assess the precise influence of Ambrose in provoking this evolution."

32 It can be observed in Shakespeare, too, as Boitani, *Gospel according to Shakespeare*, 1, notes the Bard's "syncretic juxtaposition of pagan deities and biblical God, the combination of magic and religion, the intertwining of politics and passion, and the contrast and complementariness of nature and culture, of Nature and Art."

33 Cf. Kolbet, *Augustine and the Cure of Souls*, 93: "Thus, in this way the diverse classical philosophical traditions had a unity about them for those capable of understanding it—a unity more clearly visible in the writings of Plotinus .... For Augustine to believe that this tradition had resources to care for the soul is not to say that it was capable of doing so independently of Christianity .... As he strove to improve their thinking about such things by philosophical argument, he did so implying that such an exercise led to Christianity." It has happy implications for reading Scripture as well, because it too can have multiple interpretations, just as other texts can have the same meaning as Scripture. See Miles, *Augustine and the Fundamentalist's*

Daughter, 10: "Augustine professed to tolerate, even to appreciate, multiple interpretations of Scripture, so long as they did not violate Christian doctrine."

34 Cf. Garry Wills, *Saint Augustine's Conversion* (New York: Penguin, 2004) 32: "The idea that calculation cannot go with sincerity is naïve .... Augustine, in the same way, is a master of words because he sees in their paradoxes the mysteries of the Word .... The rhetorical presentation of his own turmoil is no different from his highly rhetorical presentation of the life and suffering of Jesus. He is entirely sincere in both."

35 Though the play's final speech, 5.3.392-395, is assigned to Albany in the Quarto: see Warren, "Quarto and Folio *King Lear* and the Interpretation of Albany and Edgar," 55.

36 Also invoked by Kent at 2.2.188-89; Edmund at 5.3.209.

3

The Problem of Nature

We have postponed some implications of earlier discussions to this chapter, because a big part of the claims of either *Confessions* or *King Lear* is that love and language are huge, constitutive elements of human nature. But what "human nature" means in these texts, beyond "being a talking animal that desires things" will now occupy our thoughts more specifically, as we examine how the characters talk of the "nature" of themselves and others. Are some objects of desire natural, and some unnatural or monstrous? Why? The same could be asked of speech. Is some speech natural and some unnatural? Or would artificial then be a better contrasting term to natural, in that context? And could a person be so unnatural in their desires and speech, as to be unnatural themselves? And finally, what of nature beyond the human, the natural world around us, of storms and planets, plants and animals, fields and forests? Is that world one we fully and completely inhabit, so that we, too, are part of nature, or is human nature somehow set above or in contrast to animal or inanimate nature? As above, *King Lear* is the richer text, as many characters come with many points of view on a given question, but *Confessions* is the more systematic and finally conclusive, as Augustine usually wants to present some final answer, and not just leave us with an intriguing, interesting, thought-provoking experience on which to reflect.

I tell my students early in the semester (hopefully early in their college careers, as I think it is a fundamental and simple rule to learn to follow) that a big part of understanding how to begin to approach a question is to consider what are the opposites one has in mind, for the terms one is investigating. My comment on "artificial" above points in the direction of how this might affect our current discussion. If I ask about nature, or what is natural, one should first think, "Natural, as opposed to what?" Artificial? Mechanical? Manmade? Unnatural? Abnormal? Monstrous? Deformed? Supernatural? How different would be the effect, if we read labels on food products that claimed the products contained "unnatural" or "supernatural" sweeteners or flavors, as opposed to merely "artificial"?

As we saw in the first book of *Confessions*, Augustine sees love in its most basic, simplest form, of wanting or desiring something, as the most fundamental urge of humans. For him, we are only quite secondarily political or social or reasoning animals. All those various faculties or aspects of us, all just cater to the most basic, primal urge, which is to want things. So, for example, we don't want things so we can reason or form political alliances, we form political alliances and reason, to satisfy needs or desires. And, with Augustine, we can see this primacy of desire developmentally, by observing that infants only want; they cannot reason or speak or negotiate or operate machinery or all the other things they'll learn to do (to fulfill their wants), but they are possessed of infinite desire from birth. And as Augustine proposes as he contemplates infants (since he cannot think back to when he was himself an infant and analyze that memory, the way he does many events of his life, post-infancy), the inborn desire we have is sinful (for everyone born after Adam and Eve) because it is so overwhelming and drives us to be and act utterly selfishly (and therefore, ultimately, self-destructively). If it could, it would obey no constraints, and infants display this constantly (according to Augustine). People learn self-control, but usually only in the sense of delayed gratification, not in the sense of abandoning or even lessening their desires, so this is a refinement of their sinful urge, but Augustine believes education cannot eradicate it. So to our minimal definition of "human nature," we might expand it in an Augustinian way, as, "To be a speaking animal with sinful desires."

Fine, and I think that definition would fit myself and most people, most of the time, as to our nature and the actions to which our nature drives us. And for his modern critics (and even many of his contemporaries), that definition would be enough to discount and ignore Augustine as an absurd, insufferable scold, and pessimist, possibly even neurotic or deranged. That's assuming he's not an outright hypocrite, making outlandish, judgmental demands of people he himself does not attempt to fulfill. But I must say, I seldom see him accused of that particular fault. It seems most of his critics go right for his vision of human nature as too dark and depressing to be taken seriously, if even babies are evil (so much so that they are bound for an eternity in hell, if they die unbaptized). Babies in hell? Really? One hardly feels the need to refute him, once it's established he believes that because what could be more—well, *unnatural*—than to believe such a thing (and bequeath such a belief to Christendom ever after)? Everyone loves babies; it's positively natural to do so.[1]

In a way, I could now just jump to my first point that the most basic sense of "natural" in these texts is familial love, especially between child and parent, since we see it here in our (totally natural) revulsion for Augustine's ideas. But let's not leave Augustine merely and prematurely defeated and ignored by his Pelagian (ancient or modern) attackers. Let us pause a moment, to consider that Augustine writes not just of our desires driving us to fulfill them, but he notes another outcome of our having these overwhelming desires: "You have made us and drawn us to yourself, and our heart is unquiet until it rests in you" (*Conf.* 1.1.1). In a weirdly optimistic way, Augustine thinks our desires are so enormous, constantly changing, and ever renewing themselves that although we may temporarily fulfill some of them, we can never really satisfy them; they include in our experience of them a powerful reminder of their futility and our inevitable dissatisfaction with them.[2] Merely temporarily satisfying desires, over and over, would be the most focused, undiluted form of *sinful* human life—it would be hellish, in short—but it would therefore be an intolerable experience of a real or fully human life. The fact (according to Augustine) that we are not just sinful, but also made by God and for God, would alert us, even in our sinful state, that we want or love something more—for Augustine, God; if we wish to be more broad and inclusive, let us say anything transcendent, anything that is not a "thing" that we can possess, but something beyond us in which we participate (e.g., love, beauty, justice, truth). So to be fair to Augustine, and to make our analysis more precise and accurate, we would have to expand our definition now of human nature according to Augustine, to, "To be a speaking animal, with sinful desires that do not fully satisfy it, that cause it restlessness."

So it is human nature to love and desire badly, but not so badly that we completely lose sight of what good love would be—ultimately, for Augustine, love of God, or love of a neighbor, as commanded by God—nor that we so thoroughly embrace bad love, that we completely forget its badness and the restlessness and dissatisfaction it brings us (at least, we could not forget this, long term, though we unfortunately often do for short periods of time). And though it is the angry, jealous glare of the baby, directed at another baby, that fascinates Augustine and makes us appalled at his fascination, the scene continues, moving from condemning sin, to praising God for giving life and the necessities of life:

> Your will is that I should praise you, O Lord my God, who gave life and a body to that infant; you will me to praise you who equipped him with faculties, built up his limbs, and adorned him with a distinctive shape, as we can see. You implanted in him all the urges proper to a living creature to ensure his coherence and safety; and now you command me to praise you for those gifts, and to confess to you and sing to your name, O Most High. (*Conf.* 1.7.12)

"You implanted in him all the urges proper to a living creature." So it is not the desire for food that is sinful, but the supposed desire (envy) that the other baby *not* have food.[3] The milk flowing from mother (or in this case, probably nurse maid) to child, the baby's desire for it, the woman's desire and ability to produce it, the bond and love between the two (if not, due to sin, between two feeding babies)[4]—all are from God. If envy and rage are seen between us and our peers from the moment we're born, as the paradigm of all sinful feelings and behaviors, then the love between mother and child is also seen from the beginning, seen in the very same event, and is the model of all "natural" human love (and analogous to the love between us and God, as human children to a divine parent).

The love, or lack thereof, between parent and child, is of course at the heart of *King Lear*. We have already examined the opening scene for (among other things) this dynamic. But let's focus more on filial and parental love as natural in the play (and in our analysis of it). Lear includes it in his initial demand: "Where nature doth with merit challenge" (*King Lear* 1.1.58). He claims to be measuring and rewarding a naturally occurring love that has been heightened and deepened by practice and virtue. But when the king does not get what he wants, he grotesquely withdraws his love for Cordelia[5]:

LEAR
Let it be so. Thy truth, then, be thy dower,
For by the sacred radiance of the sun,
The mysteries of Hecate and the night,
By all the operation of the orbs
From whom we do exist and cease to be,
Here I disclaim all my paternal care,
Propinquity, and property of blood,
And as a stranger to my heart and me
Hold thee from this forever. The barbarous Scythian,
Or he that makes his generation messes
To gorge his appetite, shall to my bosom
Be as well neighbored, pitied, and relieved
As thou my sometime daughter.

(*KL* 1.1.120-133)

The only possible excuse—which, to his credit, Lear tries only briefly—is to claim that one can withdraw natural affection from someone who has herself behaved so unnaturally that she has shown herself incapable and unworthy of giving or receiving such love. Toward an unnatural being, one should also behave unnaturally, the way one would toward something that only appeared human, but was not (e.g., a robot or mannequin). Lear describes Cordelia thusly to France, trying to talk him out of loving her:

LEAR
Then leave her, sir, for by the power that made me
I tell you all her wealth.—For you, great king,
I would not from your love make such a stray
To match you where I hate. Therefore beseech you
T' avert your liking a more worthier way
Than on a wretch whom Nature is ashamed
Almost t' acknowledge hers.

(*KL* 1.1.239-244)

So long as Lear holds on to that excuse, and does not own the fact that it was he who acted unnaturally, not Cordelia, then he cannot repent of the evil he has done (because he doesn't yet recognize it as evil); but as noted, he has begun to quit such abdication of responsibility and is starting to accept blame, very early in the play: "I did her wrong" (*King Lear* 1.5.24). The continued and worsening abuse from Goneril and Regan cause Lear to postpone the full realization of his failures because he is then obsessed with (partly justified) self-pity, and much less justifiable self-congratulation: "I will forget my nature. So kind a father!" (*King Lear* 1.5.32). The natural love between child and parent is exactly how Cordelia described her love for her father (*King Lear* 1.1.105-115), despite his unnatural demands on her and her sisters. And of course she proceeds to prove her natural, filial love through her actions for the rest of the play, showing that a truly natural love persists, even if the beloved acts unnaturally.

Knowing that filial love is natural, and the denial or cessation of it unnatural, Edmund can use these assumptions as part of his subterfuge against his brother and father, by feigning such loving concern for Gloucester, and accusing his brother Edgar of plotting the fratricide and parricide that Edmund himself does not mind bringing about. (He seems pretty neutral if either his male relatives live or die, so long as they are out of his way—he is greedy, selfish, uncaring, but not particularly blood-thirsty or sadistic.)

EDMUND
Persuade me to the murder of your Lordship,
But that I told him the revenging gods
'Gainst parricides did all the thunder bend,
Spoke with how manifold and strong a bond
The child was bound to th' father—sir, in fine,
Seeing how loathly opposite I stood
To his unnatural purpose, in fell motion
With his preparèd sword he charges home
My unprovided body, lanced mine arm;
And when he saw my best alarumed spirits,
Bold in the quarrel's right, roused to th' encounter,
Or whether ghasted by the noise I made,
Full suddenly he fled.

(*KL* 2.1.53-65)

When first warned by Edmund of this supposed plot, Gloucester had declared anyone guilty of such filial treachery, "Unnatural, detested, brutish/villain! Worse than brutish!" (*King Lear* 1.2.80-81). "Brutish," as in, animal-like, having a nature appropriate to some creature but not a human one. How much more heartbreaking does that make Gloucester's futile, misguided cry for help, as he sits in the middle of the stage, blinded and bleeding:

> GLOUCESTER
> All dark and comfortless! Where's my son Edmund?—
> Edmund, enkindle all the sparks of nature
> To quit this horrid act.
>
> (*KL* 3.7.103-106)

Gloucester cries out for a natural love to save him from this torture, but it is not there—at least, not from Edmund. Edgar, like Cordelia, has maintained his natural love despite his errant father's rejection of it, and like her, his love expresses itself as suffering to make his father understand such love finally.

As we saw in our first chapter, the dysfunction between Edmund and his cheating father finds a less violent parallel with Augustine's cold appraisal of his own unfaithful and (to his mind) generally unsavory father. Edmund's schemes are malicious and rapacious, while Augustine's ambition only drives him to be aloof and supercilious toward his hard-working father. Little natural affection can be found in Augustine's description of their relationship. His father seems to Augustine just a less restrained, less enlightened, more worldly, and less successful version of himself. (And to be Freudian for just one moment: clearly less deserving of mom's love than her brilliant and devoted son.) Patricius's apparent enthusiasm for grandchildren—a common enough, or dare we say, natural enough wish for a man his age—is interpreted by Augustine as the epitome of sin:

> His glee sprang from that intoxication which has blotted you, our creator, out of this world's memory and led it to love the creature instead, as it drinks the unseen wine of its perverse inclination and is dragged down to the depths. (*Conf.* 2.3.6)

And even if, on the other hand, Monica is praised throughout *Confessions*, Augustine always qualifies her desires as not sufficiently in line with God's will, even if they are more so than those of her husband or her wayward son at the time:

> Both my parents were very keen on my making progress in study: my father, because he thought next to nothing about you and only vain things about me; and my mother, because she regarded the customary course of studies as no hindrance, and even a considerable help, toward my gaining you eventually. So, at least, do I interpret their respective attitudes, as I remember them now as best I can. (*Conf.* 2.3.8)

The "urges proper to a living creature" would include filial and parental love, and such would be a natural gift of God to all people.[6] But a supernatural love of God—God's love for us being supernatural because it comes from God; our love for him being instilled and perfected by God's grace and not our own nature or merit, and therefore supernatural—is the ultimate goal and perfection for Augustine. Such a supernatural love perfects and fulfills all mortal loves finally, as Augustine says of friendships (*Conf.* 4.9.14), and of his imperfect, human parents (*Conf.* 9.13.37). But in his telling of their story, I think generations of readers have heard and felt that Augustine could not hide whatever lingering resentments there were, over the shortcomings and disappointments of natural, familial love, as well as his own embarrassment at such feelings. In some ways, it is another confirmation of Augustine's theory of our restless human nature to love, but to do so badly, that loving our parents is at one and the same time the most natural, spontaneous, undeniable part of our being, but one we find so hard to do and express rightly, once we are past the breastfeeding stage (and even at that earliest stage, feelings toward father are conflicted).[7]

Let us return to Lear's telling France that Cordelia is a "wretch whom Nature is ashamed/Almost t' acknowledge hers" (*King Lear* 1.1.243-244). As we saw in Chapter 1, France is not having any of it:

> FRANCE
> This is most strange,
> That she whom even but now was your best object,
> The argument of your praise, balm of your age,

The best, the dearest, should in this trice of time
Commit a thing so monstrous to dismantle
So many folds of favor. Sure her offense
Must be of such unnatural degree
That monsters it, or your forevouched affection
Fall into taint; which to believe of her
Must be a faith that reason without miracle
Should never plant in me.

(*KL* 1.1.245-256)

France refuses "to believe" his new beloved is "unnatural," unless something supernatural (a "miracle") forces him to. As above, France feels something is going on with the "gods" (*King Lear* 1.1.294), if he here says only a "miracle" could move him from his newfound love and respect for Cordelia. There is here again some hint that love is natural, even as it comes from and draws us toward something(s) supernatural or divine. There is also an interesting elision between familial and romantic love here.

This blending or overflowing of love from one kind (familial) to another (romantic) continues throughout the play, encompassing many more people in Lear's orbit, and other kinds of love, all of them somehow natural (and likewise, the denial or betrayal of them as unnatural).[8] Edgar's love for the king, who is also his godfather, is shown in his actions of protecting and guiding Lear, but also in exclamations, like, "O, thou side-piercing sight!" (*King Lear* 4.6.104),[9] of pained distress at seeing Lear suffer. As godson, there is some of the familial love of Cordelia, but broadened beyond those directly related by blood to a fictive kinship that is nonetheless powerful and durable.

Harder to classify is the loving familiarity between Lear and the Fool. There is the constant, affectionate banter between them, with pet names like "fool," "nuncle," "boy," "lad," traded back and forth. And again, the Fool reminds us, or is identified with, Cordelia throughout (especially if the casting moves us to see that identity), and again carries some reminiscence of the parent–child relationship (if sometimes reversed, as it often is in the parent's old age).[10] What would we even call their relationship? "Master/servant" hardly seems to capture it; neither does "friends," really (though it captures other elements of it). One amateur production I saw cast the Fool as an elderly man, as old as or older than Lear, in drag, so the effect on stage was like seeing an old married couple bickering good naturedly (and being increasingly marginalized and abused by their younger family members). As unusual as the costuming seemed at first, it quickly felt right for capturing their familiarity, and their common affliction. Whatever it is, and however one would try to depict it on stage, when they're together, they feel like they complete each other, as we said in Chapter 1, and connected to Augustine's invocation that a friend is "another self .... half one's own soul." To say something that grand and mysterious about friendship is to invite speculation on the supernatural origins of such relationships.[11]

With the devotion and love of Gloucester and Kent for Lear, we have relationships that are more clearly in the master–servant or lord–vassal category. I suppose these kinds of relationships are out of favor now, but I cannot help but admire the love between these men. And in a way, it takes us back, full circle, to the parent–child love with which we began this discussion of what is natural, because the lord–vassal is supposed to mimic or be based on the father–son relationship. Gloucester, as noted above, does not start the play as the most admirable or courageous of characters, but he quickly reaches his limit, of the cruelty he can see doled out on Lear, before he feels he has to intervene:

> GLOUCESTER
> Alack, alack, Edmund, I like not this
> unnatural dealing. When I desired their leave that I
> might pity him, they took from me the use of mine
> own house, charged me on pain of perpetual
> displeasure neither to speak of him, entreat for
> him, or any way sustain him.
>
> EDMUND
> Most savage and unnatural.
>
> (*KL* 3.3.1-7)

The savagery being visited upon Lear is not "discreet proceeding" (*King Lear* 1.4.219), or "discretion" (*King Lear* 2.4.167), as his own flesh and blood would have it. But this lecherous, not too bright underling "gets" that what is happening is "unnatural," and it spurs him to bravery and sacrifice for his lord.[12] And as above, Edmund is shrewd enough to play along for now and label it similarly: again, language for him and the other evil characters is useful, when brute force and violence cannot prudently or effectively be used.

And on the matter of such love between those of different ranks being natural, Kent's description when meeting his lord while disguised seems to underline how natural, instinctive, and immediate is their connection:

KENT
No, sir, but you have that in your countenance
which I would fain call master.

LEAR
What's that?

KENT
Authority.

(*KL* 1.4.28-31)

Even if it is in some way an act on Kent's part (see our Chapter 2), he describes here (apparently convincingly) a bromance version of love at first sight. And really, as I thought about such devotion, the sheer number of bromances in the Western canon began to impress itself anew upon me—Enkidu and Gilgamesh, Patroclus and Achilles, David and Jonathan, Beowulf and Wiglaf, Dante and Virgil (my favorite), Ishmael and Queequeg. And in Shakespeare's hands, with some of the comedies (*As You Like It*, *Twelfth Night*), we see again the elision of seemingly different kinds of love, this time from bromance to heterosexual romance.[13] As academics we perhaps delight too much in making fine distinctions (and I will continue a devotion to such tasks), but we should also consider that different species of love also bear some generic resemblance and formal connection to each other. Alas, the Fool observes this on the evil end of the spectrum:

FOOL
Shalt see thy other daughter will use thee kindly,
for, though she's as like this as a crab's like an
apple, yet I can tell what I can tell.

LEAR
What canst tell, boy?

FOOL
She will taste as like this as a crab does to a crab.
(*KL* 1.5.14-18)

We can surely distinguish all sorts of gradations and nuances of unnatural evil between the villains in *King Lear*, but the labels would still be meaningful and show we sense their shared lineage and effects.[14] So too in far happier ways, the connections between parents and children, or romantic partners, or non-sexual partners, or other natural relationships of compassion and kindness can all be called love and share many characteristics, origins, and results.

As we conclude this discussion of how natural love is, and how utterly unnatural—and I think in this case we can specify we mean unnatural in the sense of monstrous, perverse—it is to deny or betray those we love (or are supposed to love), we can underline how close *Confessions* and *King Lear* are on nature and love, while distinguishing them on some points. The two texts are quite close in showing the various dysfunctions of familial love (while insisting parent–child love is the model for all others). Cheating fathers are in both, while mothers fail in different ways—by being absent in *King Lear*, or by sometimes smothering in *Confessions*. Disobedient children drive the conflicts in both. Earthly ambition for achievements and life outside the family threaten the family relationships in both. Romantic relationships are much less prominent in either text. France's love for Cordelia is powerful and positive, is somehow connected in his mind to "gods," and it enables her to try to save her father. But the marriage itself is barely an issue or described in the play, and France himself never reappears after declaring his love. Augustine's love for the mother of his child finally is abandoned as first incompatible with his career and financial ambitions, but then those too are abandoned for his new commitment to God, and he is left with celibacy (what many would consider the most unnatural arrangement possible), as the only way he feels he can live this new life. But then the most natural, noble kind of loving relationship in both texts is some kind of committed, non-romantic relationship—what I have flippantly called "bromance" in *King Lear* but if one reflects on the literary antecedents I listed, I think they are worthy of emulation and a nobler label (whatever that would be). In *King Lear* these are mostly between lord and vassal, except for the mysterious bond between Lear and the Fool. In *Confessions* they are more the mutual friendships between males of equal status (Augustine and Alypius, Nebridius, or the youthful friends described in Book Four). It is these friendships that Augustine thinks can be, should be, "in God," and therefore are in their own way, holy, a natural relationship that takes on supernatural or divine implications and direction.[15]

If love is or can be natural in both texts, let us consider next that Nature itself might be a deity—as love and nature were goddesses for Greeks and Romans, and even for the secular, personified and called upon by poets. This is how Edmund calls upon Nature in his soliloquy:

EDMUND
Thou, Nature, art my goddess. To thy law
My services are bound. Wherefore should I
Stand in the plague of custom, and permit
The curiosity of nations to deprive me
For that I am some twelve or fourteen moonshines
Lag of a brother? why "bastard"? Wherefore "base,"
When my dimensions are as well compact,
My mind as generous and my shape as true
As honest madam's issue? Why brand they us
With "base," with "baseness," "bastardy," "base," "base,"
Who, in the lusty stealth of nature, take
More composition and fierce quality
Than doth within a dull, stale, tired bed
Go to th' creating a whole tribe of fops
Got 'tween asleep and wake? Well then,
Legitimate Edgar, I must have your land.
Our father's love is to the bastard Edmund
As to th' legitimate. Fine word, "legitimate."
Well, my legitimate, if this letter speed
And my invention thrive, Edmund the base
Shall top th' legitimate. I grow, I prosper.
Now, gods, stand up for bastards!

(*KL* 1.2.1-23)

And unlike France merely calling upon "gods" at the mention of his love, Edmund pledges himself to this goddess. But he will serve her instead of what? As we began our discussion of nature, what it is contrasted with makes all the difference to understanding what a thing is. Edmund spends most of his speech deriding the assumptions and effects of "custom" and "nations." He begins with the unfair disadvantages these entities have heaped upon him: again, think back to the humiliating opening scene with his father and Kent, and imagine a lifetime of such incidents, and much worse, since the exchange we witnessed is how Edmund is treated by someone who claims to love him![16] And for all his faults, Gloucester seems to mean this—he does love Edmund (and Edmund's mother)—he is just really bad at showing it. Consider even that in the Quarto the stage directions don't give Edmund's name, but just his label, "Bastard." Edmund's word associations are brilliant and bitter here, and it's probably the best speech in the play by a character other than Lear. People call Edmund bastard, and then broaden that legal term to a moral one, calling him base (vulgar, unevolved, evil). An unlawful, immoral event before his birth now determines the legal and moral judgments people make of him, and this will continue unabated his whole life. Who would not pledge themselves to a new deity (or an old one, if this is some return to a preexisting goddess who had been supplanted), if the categories of the currently existing world order (supposedly mandated and upheld by the gods or a God) have been so unfair and detrimental to oneself?[17]

So if Edmund abandons the world that uses such labels as "bastard" and "base," what does his new goddess Nature promise? How will she and her followers judge people, or what behaviors or qualities will they honor and reward? Edmund claims they will be based on objective qualities—"dimensions," "mind," and "shape"—and not the hypocritical criteria of who is "honest," to determine the made-up, misleading, legal label of "legitimate." For Edmund, that becomes the totally unsurprising contrast (because it has been a contrast so constant, painful, and detrimental to him his whole life), but to us very shocking, that the opposite of Nature is (human) law. Nature herself has a law, that Edmund now claims to follow, but its code is individual survival by any means. Edmund in essence claims to be the result of a totally natural process that is only impeded by human custom and unnaturally punished by human laws: his father stepped out of a "dull, stale, tired" marriage, to exercise his "lust" and "stealth," and the resulting offspring (Edmund) therefore has "more composition and fierce quality." Interesting (and somewhat confusing) that Edmund even includes in his description that his father's love for him is part of this more natural arrangement, and shows that any preference for Edgar is undeserved, unfair, unnatural. Even Edmund believes love is natural, but it is love in some biological, not ethical or emotional or even conscious or deliberate sense. His father loves him by passing on his "fierce quality" to him, so Edmund should properly acknowledge and spread this love, not by being kind to either his father or brother, but by ruthlessly eradicating them,[18] so as to perpetuate the more powerful, hardier elements of the Gloucester line (and even merging it, politically and biologically, with the Lear line; though Edmund can't have foreseen that part yet, when it presents itself, it would at that point confirm everything he's done for Nature and in the name of natural love).

Edmund's devotion to a new goddess, Nature, against the old gods who have upheld a human society that humiliated and disadvantaged him, is fully understandable. But surprising then that shortly after, Lear also, who has his whole life benefited from and rose to the top of human society and law, also calls upon this goddess, Nature. Something must differ in their concepts of Nature, so let us unpack Lear's. As Goneril and Regan's treatment of their father degenerates, Lear curses them in increasingly violent, obscene terms:

LEAR
Woe that too late repents!—O, sir, are you come?
Is it your will? Speak, sir.—Prepare my horses.
Some exit.
Ingratitude, thou marble-hearted fiend,
More hideous when thou show'st thee in a child
Than the sea monster!

ALBANY
Pray, sir, be patient.

LEAR, *to Goneril*
Detested kite, thou liest.
My train are men of choice and rarest parts,

That all particulars of duty know
And in the most exact regard support
The worships of their name. O most small fault,
How ugly didst thou in Cordelia show,
Which, like an engine, wrenched my frame of nature
From the fixed place, drew from my heart all love
And added to the gall! O Lear, Lear, Lear!
He strikes his head.
Beat at this gate that let thy folly in
And thy dear judgment out. Go, go, my people.
(*KL* 1.4.267-285)

Nature here is not a goddess, but just Lear's nature, and he laments that Cordelia "wrenched [it] ... From the fixed place." When his nature was thus wrenched from its foundation, Lear ceased to love Cordelia—i.e., loving her was natural, ceasing to love her is unnatural. Since he has not yet fully accepted his own blame and absolved Cordelia, he still thinks this is her "fault," but he also "repents" of some mistake on his part, a lack of "judgment" that made him act according to "folly." Lear's folly was to put himself at the mercy of his other two daughters—foolish because they have no mercy, and increasingly feel empowered and emboldened not to restrain or hide their rapaciousness, lust, or cruelty. So here he can only lash out verbally at Goneril, calling her "fiend," "sea monster," and "kite." But to call one's own daughter such things is itself unnatural, and Lear's only excuse (partly justified here with Goneril, not at all with Cordelia) is that she is being unnatural toward him.

So Lear starts his cursing as an unnatural act ("wrenched my frame of nature/From the fixed place"), in response to unnatural treatment by his daughters. It is a continuation of his foolish cursing of Cordelia and Kent in the first scene, and therefore he still includes Cordelia as one of the instigators of this unnatural treatment of himself, though Lear is painfully and belatedly becoming aware that her candor was not unnatural nor evil, now that he sees what real evil is like, with the carping demands, casual disrespect, and increasingly overt cruelty of Goneril and Regan. But Lear then moves on from retaliatory unnatural behavior, to calling upon Nature herself to do his bidding and endorse his behavior and curses:

LEAR
It may be so, my lord.—
Hear, Nature, hear, dear goddess, hear!
Suspend thy purpose if thou didst intend
To make this creature fruitful.
Into her womb convey sterility.
Dry up in her the organs of increase,
And from her derogate body never spring
A babe to honor her. If she must teem,
Create her child of spleen, that it may live
And be a thwart disnatured torment to her.
Let it stamp wrinkles in her brow of youth,
With cadent tears fret channels in her cheeks,
Turn all her mother's pains and benefits
To laughter and contempt, that she may feel
How sharper than a serpent's tooth it is
To have a thankless child.—Away, away!

(*KL* 1.4.288-303)

The curse has amplified and personalized considerably, even as Lear attempts to justify such violence, and not see it all as his own descent into increasingly unnatural behavior, in the face of an unnatural world and the people in it. He goes on to intensify it around this concept, of a father's natural love now having turned into something terrible:

LEAR
I'll tell thee. *To Goneril.* Life and death! I am ashamed
That thou hast power to shake my manhood thus,
That these hot tears, which break from me perforce,
Should make thee worth them. Blasts and fogs upon thee!
Th' untented woundings of a father's curse
Pierce every sense about thee!

(*KL* 1.4.311-318)

Now his curses are not just stock insults of comparing the hated person to animals that are deemed unclean and unnatural, but are very specific to his situation. He calls down on Goneril what he believes is the awful treatment she has meted out on him—filial ingratitude—with the same effects it is having on him—"torment," "wrinkles in her brow," and "tears." But the latter transforms into something much more disturbing, the further he goes. Lear feels weeping is effeminate, so to call it down on Goneril would not hurt her the way it does him, by making her behave in some way against her female nature. No, that is what requires the goddess's supernatural intervention, in his now tortured mind, calling down on his daughter a de-feminizing of her that would somehow match, balance, and avenge what he feels is his own emasculation.[19]

Lear's idea of nature, therefore, has degenerated from an idea of natural love that he foolishly rejected; this is ultimately the idea he will have to return to, to accept his guilt, and love rightly again, however briefly. But under Goneril's harangue, Lear has fantasized a goddess Nature far worse than Edmund's merely neutral, amoral Darwinian force that is (or should be) preferred to hypocritical, vicious human laws. Lear's goddess Nature is just what every monotheist is accused of worshipping at some point—a giant, cosmic version of himself, so powerful it can do things the believer or worshiper cannot, things for which it can't be held accountable, a being whose whims and jealous rages are all supposedly justified, though only because there is no one strong enough to oppose it.[20] Edmund imagines a Being who will approve of his predations (that he'll call fierceness or potency); Lear fantasizes a Being who can sadistically torture his enemies because he is too impotent to do so himself, enemies he has foolishly provoked and empowered to harm himself (and unfortunately, many others). The two men's concepts are only similar in their believing this is somehow fair or just or natural.

This then is the most blasphemous and idolatrous these two characters will become, imagining Nature approves of everything he does (Edmund), or imagining it can avenge all the harm that has come upon him because of his own mistakes or sins or crimes (Lear). We will consider Edmund's end at the conclusion of this chapter, but let us look now at Lear's development. As we have noted, he has inklings of his own guilt very early, but the evil of Goneril and Regan (far greater and more cunning and deliberate than his own) puts him on a detour of self-pity. But on the heath with Edgar and Gloucester, Lear makes progress on exactly this issue of finally denying his own self-deification:

LEAR
Ha! Goneril with a white beard? They flattered
me like a dog and told me I had the white hairs in

> my beard ere the black ones were there. To say "ay"
> and "no" to everything that I said "ay" and "no" to
> was no good divinity. When the rain came to wet me
> once and the wind to make me chatter, when the
> thunder would not peace at my bidding, there I
> found 'em, there I smelt 'em out. Go to. They are
> not men o' their words; they told me I was everything.
> 'Tis a lie. I am not ague-proof.
>
> (*KL* 4.6.115-124)

So much painful, necessary realization is in these lines, even as they combine the imaginary ("Goneril with a white beard?"), with flashbacks that are all too real. Lear now knows Nature does not do his "bidding." He accepts the emptiness of language, and admits his own error, fallibility, and limitations.

The scene is so convincing and harrowing, however, because it contains so much of the old Lear, still, even as it careens from realization to denial to dark humor and back to realization. In his next speech he is back to asserting his power, "Ay, every inch a king" (*King Lear* 4.6.127), and grotesquely back to describing a hallucinatory horror show of female sexuality (though this time, significantly, not as a curse upon it, but a bitter celebration of it). But then he is back to another apposite, painful observation about his former life:

> LEAR
> What, art mad? A man may see how this world
> goes with no eyes. Look with thine ears. See how
> yond justice rails upon yond simple thief. Hark in
> thine ear. Change places and, handy-dandy, which
> is the justice, which is the thief? Thou hast seen a
> farmer's dog bark at a beggar?
>
> GLOUCESTER
> Ay, sir.
>
> LEAR
> And the creature run from the cur? There thou
> might'st behold the great image of authority: a
> dog's obeyed in office.
>
> (*KL* 4.6.165-174)

This takes us from one end of Lear's painful education to the other, from him asserting identity with some idolatrous Nature that is just a hypostasis of his sinful desires for revenge, writ large, to a crushing self-identification with a less than human (canine) reality, that at the supposed, pretended height of his power, he was no more authoritative or right or just than a barking dog.[21]

With Lear's depth of sin or height of idolatry in imagining himself as God, we see a scenario much like Augustine's conception of how all sin devolves into idolatry of ourselves. Whatever we might imagine we love (sex, money, power, etc.), for Augustine it all finally comes down to loving ourselves instead of God. Here our problem of comparison between the two texts would be with the incident Augustine chooses as his epitome of sin. If any normal reader is left bemused at the idea of sinful babies, then the famous pear tree theft in Book Two is confounding for other reasons. The idea that babies are sinful strikes us (I would hope) as absurd on its face. The idea that teenagers are nasty, selfish, stupid little monsters seems much easier to accept (either from observation of them in the wild, or honest recollection of one's own antics as such). I remember the first time I taught *Confessions* at Villanova. When we discussed the passage in class, one young man volunteered that he could sort of understand the incident, how motiveless and unappealing it was, when Augustine looked back on it. He related how, very similarly to Augustine and his "nasty lads" (*Conf.* 2.4.9), he and some friends had stolen watermelons, and to destroy the evidence, had eaten all of them, to the point of feeling sick and not at all pleased with their foul deed (but definitely feeling it was foul at that point). Someone else in the class asked when this had occurred. I at least thought the former thief would answer when he was ten or eleven. But he said, "Oh. Back in July." A wonderful few moments of hearty laughter followed, and the whole incident nicely illustrates the problem with the story. That it is a description of something sinful (or at least, imprudent or indulgent) is undeniable (unlike the evil, glaring babies passage). But that it is something as serious as Augustine makes it out to be, and not just something at which to laugh, is much harder to comprehend.

But perhaps its ubiquity and ordinariness are why Augustine chooses it. Augustine is convinced of, and trying to show us, the universality of sin, after all, not the exceptionality or enormity of it (even though his description does veer into the hyperbolic at times), so we should be looking for it in everyday events to which we all can relate. Augustine wants us to see, even in his childish prank (and therefore, even in our childish pranks), something that partook of self-idolatry:

> With regard to my theft, then: what did I love in it, and in what sense did I imitate my Lord, even if only with vicious perversity? Did the pleasure I sought lie in breaking the law at least in that sneaky way, since I was unable to do so with any show of strength? Was I, in truth a prisoner, trying to simulate a crippled sort of freedom, attempting a shady parody of omnipotence by getting away with something forbidden? How like that servant of yours who fled from his Lord and hid in the shadows! What rottenness, what a misshapen life! Rather a hideous pit of death! To do what was wrong simply because it was wrong—could I have found pleasure in that? (*Conf.* 2.6.14)

A "crippled sort of freedom" and "a shady parody of omnipotence," here especially sound more appropriate to Lear than the teenage Augustine, but the claimed resemblance is there. In their very different idioms, our two texts both depict sin as ultimately a kind of self-idolatry, claiming power and infallibility one could never have.

Edmund's soliloquy on Nature gives way to his starting to enact his plans against his father and brother. All of these plans rely on his observations and evaluations of them, as he summarizes at the end of the scene:

> EDMUND
> I do serve you in this business. *Edgar exits.*
> A credulous father and a brother noble,
> Whose nature is so far from doing harms
> That he suspects none; on whose foolish honesty
> My practices ride easy. I see the business.
> Let me, if not by birth, have lands by wit.
> All with me's meet that I can fashion fit.
> (*KL* 1.2.186-192)

The "nature" of Gloucester and Edgar is just not equipped to deal with treachery and deceit.[22] Gloucester is "credulous" and Edgar is even "noble" (unpacked by Edmund as meaning "far from doing harms"), but these qualities are not sufficient against "wit," if that intellect puts no limits on itself, and is willing to do and say anything "fit" (i.e., anything necessary to accomplishing its ends). It is an interesting contrast to the Lear plot, where the king had prepared a scheme to contain his deceitful, hypocritical daughters, but was completely disarmed by the unexpectedly laconic candor of Cordelia; Gloucester and Edgar in the other plot are taken in by the glib Edmund, never having any plans of their own and just making it up as they go, throughout the play. Lear is armed against some outside threats but not against his own shortcomings; Gloucester and Edgar seem more intrinsically vulnerable to a hostile outside world.

Gloucester has his own way of thinking of and dealing with this hostile outside world, as he describes to Edmund, as Edmund's planted suspicions take hold in his mind:

> GLOUCESTER
> These late eclipses in the sun and moon
> portend no good to us. Though the wisdom of
> nature can reason it thus and thus, yet nature finds
> itself scourged by the sequent effects. Love cools,
> friendship falls off, brothers divide; in cities, mutinies;
> in countries, discord; in palaces, treason; and
> the bond cracked 'twixt son and father. This villain
> of mine comes under the prediction: there's son
> against father. The King falls from bias of nature:
> there's father against child. We have seen the best of
> our time. Machinations, hollowness, treachery, and
> all ruinous disorders follow us disquietly to our
> graves.—Find out this villain, Edmund. It shall
> lose thee nothing. Do it carefully.—And the noble
> and true-hearted Kent banished! His offense, honesty!
> 'Tis strange. *He exits.*
>
> (*KL* 1.2.109-124)

If above we saw Lear and Augustine attempting to assert a God-like, impious control over the universe and other people, as their besetting sin or character flaw, here we see Gloucester at the other extreme, fretting over his (and everyone's?) loss of agency and freedom, as they are at the mercy of the powers of "eclipses," and of a "nature" both totally beyond human control and at war with itself ("Though the wisdom of/nature can reason it thus and thus, yet nature finds/itself scourged by the sequent effects"). Exactly as we saw above, love is the essential part of human nature, and Gloucester very much agrees here. But when he describes people ceasing to love, he does not judge it harshly as Lear did, as some hideous, unnatural act the person has chosen, and for which he or she should be cursed and punished, but more like an accident, like unfortunately catching a cold. Gloucester's conception here is much more passive: such unloving acts are brought upon people, they "fall" into them, or such calamities "follow" them as an inevitable part of mortal existence. Lear grotesquely avoids responsibility by blaming Goneril and Regan for a situation he engineered and foolishly put into action. (And saying this in no way excuses or even lessens their monstrous behavior and guilt.) Gloucester saw in his adultery only a funny story to recount to other noblemen, not something of which to be ashamed or for which to apologize (to either Edgar or Edmund or their mothers). And when he sees far worse, more violent and destructive behavior starting to be unleashed here, he also does not connect it to any personal responsibility, but to the influences of celestial, not human, bodies. From very different assumptions about how people and the world work, the men very similarly conclude they are not to blame. Before we turn to consider Augustine's rather longstanding dabbling in astrology, let's pause on this issue of responsibility, and how belief in some kind of forces outside the human (fate, Devil, Nature, stars, etc.), exerting control or influence over us, tends to find its adherents, not because of any evidence (whatever such evidence could be, really), but because of its preferred explanatory value for our bad behavior:

> It still seemed to me that it is not we who sin, but some other nature within us that is responsible. My pride was gratified at being exculpated by this theory: when I had done something wrong it was pleasant to avoid having to confess I had done it, a confession that would have given you a chance to heal this soul of mine that had sinned against you. On the contrary, I liked to excuse myself and lay the blame on some other force that was

> with me but was not myself. But in truth it was all myself. My impious ideas had set up a division, pitting me against myself, and my sin was the more incurable for my conviction that I was not a sinner. (*Conf.* 5.10.18)

It is one of the points on which Augustine is withering and relentless in his self-examination. It is a point on which most of us could be much more detached, thinking how some kind of dualism is not that incredible of a belief, nor one with such dire moral implications. If there are evil forces out there (or in here, inside us) attacking us, we are still called upon to fight them. And I suppose on the matter of its logic, Augustine can be detached and objective. But his analysis is so honest, admitting that people (starting with himself) do not believe things just because they're logically compelling, or aesthetically pleasing, or confirmed by outside proof, or whatever other convenient or congratulatory things we claim for our beliefs. He doesn't even try such pedestrian explanations as peer pressure or the weight and force of tradition (since he is at that point in his life "shopping around" for a religion or philosophy). Augustine remains insistently individualistic, dissecting his motives, and admits he believed things because he found them soothing; they kept him from inconveniently having to change beliefs or behavior (even if they caused him a great deal of mental discomfort for their illogic, and that point is crucial, for their eventual abandonment).

On this issue of belief in astrology (forces of nature), as based in or leading to an abdication of responsibility, Edmund is perfectly in line with Augustine in his mockery of such an outlook:

> EDMUND
> This is the excellent foppery of the world, that
> when we are sick in fortune (often the surfeits of
> our own behavior) we make guilty of our disasters
> the sun, the moon, and stars, as if we were villains
> on necessity; fools by heavenly compulsion; knaves,
> thieves, and treachers by spherical predominance;
> drunkards, liars, and adulterers by an enforced
> obedience of planetary influence; and all that we
> are evil in, by a divine thrusting on. An admirable
> evasion of whoremaster man, to lay his goatish
> disposition on the charge of a star! My father
> compounded with my mother under the Dragon's

> tail, and my nativity was under Ursa Major, so that it
> follows I am rough and lecherous. Fut, I should
> have been that I am, had the maidenliest star in the
> firmament twinkled on my bastardizing.
>
> (*KL* 1.2.125-140)

It should be noted, however, that when Augustine condemns this outlook of "admirable evasion," it is first and most loudly in his own case. When Edmund here derides it, it is in the context of mocking the father who has humiliated him his whole life, and whom he now plans to (at a minimum) deceive into hating and disowning his brother, and whom he quickly abandons to unbelievable torture because it benefits him. For Augustine to admit years later that he believed absurd things seems like honest self-criticism. For Edmund to attack absurd beliefs he doesn't share, just seems like him piling on a father whom he already finds distasteful and boorish and inconvenient for many other reasons.

Even more revealing, however, is which parts of Edmund's critique are true, and which are themselves self-serving. His first observation is that our misfortunes are misnamed as such, whether the blame is laid on the doorsteps of stars, or on a wheel of fortune that revolves and carries us with it. Edmund claims the more rational conclusion (and it is borne out by most every event of the play) that the things that happen to us are most "often the surfeits of/our own behavior." He then goes further, and enumerates a list of actions that are not done to us, but by us—lying, stealing, treachery, drinking, pimping, adultery (if there were any doubt whom he has in mind with this attack). That some events are outside our control is undeniable; the weather is as uncontrolled by us as are the motions of the stars, and it is much less reliable and predictable, and affects us much more immediately. But to elide the weather with what I choose to do seems an "admirable evasion" at best—more like deliberate confusing of two unrelated, dissimilar phenomena. But Edmund then ends his speech with something very much like that, claiming that he is as nasty as he wants to be, not because of a star, no, but because of his "bastardizing" (something as outside his control as the motions of the stars). To say, "I'm going to act like a cruel, uncaring bastard; I have no control over it," is an evasion, whether one blames one's nativity horoscope, or one's father's actions. So Edmund has his own functional equivalent for explaining whatever he does not want to take blame for. It is refreshingly modern,

Freudian, psychological, and doesn't reek of superstition, the way astrology does, but it seems no less evasive and dishonest, as to responsibility. Everything old is new again, indeed.

As above on feigning filial love in order to dupe his father and brother, Edmund has no qualms about pretending belief in astrology when Edgar shows up:

> EDGAR
> How now, brother Edmund, what serious contemplation
> are you in?
>
> EDMUND
> I am thinking, brother, of a prediction I read
> this other day, what should follow these eclipses.
>
> EDGAR
> Do you busy yourself with that?
>
> EDMUND
> I promise you, the effects he writes of succeed
> unhappily, as of unnaturalness between the
> child and the parent, death, dearth, dissolutions of
> ancient amities, divisions in state, menaces and
> maledictions against king and nobles, needless diffidences,
> banishment of friends, dissipation of cohorts,
> nuptial breaches, and I know not what.
>
> EDGAR
> How long have you been a sectary
> astronomical?
>
> EDMUND
> Come, come, when saw you my father last?
>
> (*KL* 1.2.145-159)

Interestingly, Edgar does not seem taken in by this part of the ruse. He twice expresses surprise at Edmund's interest in astrology, and Edmund drops that part of his deception. Perhaps labelling Gloucester "credulous" and Edgar "noble" are rather precise here by Edmund. Gloucester is more gullible than Edgar, especially in matters of superstition. Edgar is "noble," unable to conceive of harming others, and therefore he doesn't do a good job defending himself against such harmful schemes, but he is not prone to believe in things as silly as astrology. Neither Edmund nor Edgar provides any real refutation of astrology (nor does Gloucester provide any confirmation, other than all the bad things happening around them). Edmund objects to the abdication of responsibility implicit in it (and then substitutes his own way to avoid blame); Edgar just seems uninterested in or incredulous of such "contemplation."

Augustine, as we have seen, has his own daddy issues, of which he allows us glimpses in *Confessions* (though more often by omissions and silence, than explicit statements). On astrology, however, he is as honest and explicit as he is with discussing his Manichaean beliefs.

> I made no move whatever to break off my habit of consulting those charlatans whom people call "mathematicians," for I took the view that no sacrifice was being offered by them, nor any prayer addressed to spirits in the practice of divination. Nonetheless true Christian piety is consistent with its own principles in rejecting and condemning astrology. It is good to confess to you .... When people say, "The sky is responsible for your sin, so you cannot avoid it," or "Venus did this, or Saturn, or Mars," they invalidate our whole salvation. They are suggesting that human beings are guiltless—humans who are flesh and blood and putrid pride!—and that the fault lies with the creator and controller of sky and stars. And who is this? You, our God, sweetness and the fount of justice, who will repay each of us as our actions deserve, and do not disdain a broken and humbled heart. (*Conf.* 4.3.4)

It is interesting that Augustine's main reason for patronizing those who cast horoscopes is some fastidiousness about what is permissible for a Christian. Merely looking for predictions from some source other than God seems to him at this time not necessarily forbidden, as long as it involves neither worship ("no sacrifice being offered"), nor necromancy ("nor any prayer addressed to spirits in the practice of divination," see Deut. 18:11; Lev. 19:31). One can see his point: if one were categorically forbidden from consulting with "experts" who examined created beings in order to make predictions about the future, then weather forecasting would be equally unlawful. But then Augustine hits on exactly the same criticism we saw from Edmund in order to condemn astrology: it is a silly way to avoid responsibility. Augustine takes it much further than Edmund, who has nowhere shown any concern about "invalidat[ing] our whole salvation." Augustine even connects it with blasphemy explicitly: if one avoids guilt oneself, and puts it on the stars, then one has put the blame ultimately on the creator of the stars ("the fault lies with the creator and controller of sky and stars. And who is this? You, our God").

It is curious, then, that Augustine sticks with astrology as long as he does ("I made no move whatever to break off my habit of consulting those charlatans"). Perhaps if he confined his queries just to outside matters (like the weather or travel conditions or other matters usually put off on chance or fortune), and didn't look to the stars to excuse his own bad behavior, Augustine could justify the practice (though he seems aware of the difficulties it raises). But then that raises the problem we did not see addressed anywhere in *King Lear*: this is to consider whether or not astrology works, on some factual level (let alone all the theoretical questions it raises of free will or theodicy), whether or not its predictions are accurate. Augustine repeatedly expresses much more interest in this issue than does any character in *King Lear*: "I asked him how, in that case, it came about that astrologers could often make predictions which proved true. He gave the best answer available, saying that this was due to chance, a force prevalent throughout nature" (*Conf.* 4.3.5). It is astrology's accuracy to which Augustine returns several times, so it apparently bothered him, in both ways—that predictions based on horoscopes were correct too often to completely discount them, but too seldom (and based on too unreliable or undefined a foundation) to rely on them. Again, my vantage point in the midst of a twenty-first-century plague seems quite similar, in that I see plenty of seemingly intelligent, reasonable people, many of them college educated, all of them using devices (cars, televisions, computers) created by modern technology, but who simultaneously embrace holistic medicine, smudging, homeopathy, chakras, and many other such practices. If pressed, I think they or Augustine have an unassailable response, "It can't hurt" (so long as they are also using all other means available to improve their situation).

Augustine also has an interesting and influential experience of astronomy, in addition to astrology. If astrologers made highly dubious claims about what eclipses or conjunctions or comets meant, they could at least base their claims on extremely accurate data about those phenomena, unlike the Manichees:

> For all that, I kept in mind many true conclusions which they had drawn from creation itself, and I saw that these could be verified by calculation, by observing the succession of the seasons and by the visible evidence of the stars. I then compared them with the assertions of Mani, who had written voluminously (and incoherently) on these subjects. What I read there was confirmed neither by any rational account of solstices and equinoxes and eclipses, nor by anything else of this kind that I had learned from books of secular philosophy. (*Conf.* 5.3.6)

Augustine's abandoning the Manichees was to some extent "data driven"—many others had accurate data about the movements of celestial bodies, while the Manichees said things that were verifiably untrue at the physical, visual, factual level. Augustine always seems more interested in their theoretical problems about the origin of evil, or the nature of God, but of course we can't decide on those matters, based on fact, by consulting what we can see or measure of physical entities. But Augustine cannot completely ignore the less fraught but much more certain questions about physical reality, which can be seen and measured, and therefore claims about it can really be proved or disproved. And on that score, the astrologers are on a firmer, more trustworthy ground than the Manichees[23]: they have accurate data, which they then interpret in ways that are at least sometimes true.

It is only upon hearing of a very elaborate experiment related to him by a friend (so it's not quite ocular proof, Augustine still has to have faith in the reporting) that Augustine considers astrology finally untrue enough that he can give up on it completely. His friend Firminus tells of how when he was born, an enslaved woman nearby was also giving birth. Both Firminus's father and the slaveowner were very interested in astrology, so had arranged to inform one another when people (or even animals) gave birth in their households, so their horoscopes could be calculated with great accuracy. Firminus relates the events of the night of his own birth:

> It happened like this. As the women went into labor the two friends sent word to each other to let each know what was happening at the other's house, and held messengers in readiness who would announce to each the birth of the child as soon as it occurred. It was easy for them to arrange for instantaneous announcement, since each was master in his own domain. So, Firminus related, the two sets of messengers were dispatched, and met at a point exactly halfway between the two houses, which meant that neither of the friends could assign a different position of the stars, or record any different moment of time. Yet Firminus was born in easy circumstances among his own relatives, and pursued quite a brilliant career in the world making money and advancing in rank, while that slave-boy went on serving his masters, with no alleviation whatever of the yoke his status imposed on him. Firminus, who knew him, testified to the fact. As soon as I heard this story, which, in view of the narrator's character, I believed, my obstinate resistance was completely overcome and dropped away. (*Conf.* 7.6.8-9)

Augustine goes on to consider the case of twins (*Conf.* 7.6.10), who obviously have the same horoscope, but don't live identical lives. Augustine mentions the specific, biblical pair of Jacob and Esau, who were very different in disposition and in the events of their lives. However suggestive any of these individually, the overall observation that many people must have the exact same horoscope and are most likely not all experiencing the same things seems convincing enough to Augustine for him to abandon this idea of using nature to predict events in human lives.

But if this nature outside ourselves, the natural world, cannot be predicted, nor called upon to do our bidding, this takes us back to reconsider human nature. What does it mean to live in such a world? What kind of human nature would be equipped for such hostility (or at least indifference) from the rest of the natural world? Human nature is weak, frail, and dependent, and this is made most clear as the hostility of the physical world is intensified. On this diagnosis (if not her evil conclusions), Regan is quite right:

> REGAN
> O sir, you are old.
> Nature in you stands on the very verge

Of his confine. You should be ruled and led
By some discretion that discerns your state
Better than you yourself. Therefore, I pray you
That to our sister you do make return.
Say you have wronged her.

(*KL* 2.4.164-170)

The noble Kent gives a similar description of human nature as weak and in need of assistance:

KENT
Oppressèd nature sleeps.
This rest might yet have balmed thy broken sinews,
Which, if convenience will not allow,
Stand in hard cure.

(*KL* 3.6.104-107)

Gloucester also exclaims on such a devastated nature, when he realizes it is the former king he is talking to, in the depths of both their sufferings:

GLOUCESTER
O, let me kiss that hand!

LEAR
Let me wipe it first; it smells of mortality.

GLOUCESTER
O ruined piece of nature!

(*KL* 4.6.147-149)

And Lear seems, with his refusal of obeisance and mocking affirmation of mortality, to be far along now in learning his rightful, natural place in the world. Regan believes such weakness as is intrinsic to our nature and compounded by age or abuse is not a cause for compassion, love, or assistance, but only a signal the weakened person can now be used and hurt with impunity, with no fear of reprisal. Kent and Gloucester, on the other hand, take the same idea of nature as an occasion to show love and care, as they do throughout the play, usually most focused on Lear's physical safety and well-being (the Fool being more attuned to his master's mental and spiritual maladies). But this way of speaking of nature comes out most explicitly and repeatedly in the scenes on the heath—i.e., scenes taking place not in the artificial world of castles and society, maps and treaties, arranged marriages and hidden intrigues, but out in the natural world when it is in the grips of uncontrollable violence, a place where love is most urgently needed and given, because the suffering and vulnerability of human nature are at their greatest.[24]

If Regan is right on some level about human nature, her cruelty toward such inevitable, human weakness means that Lear's fear of admitting such a weakened nature in himself is not just fragile male ego: it is an attempt to survive a real assault on himself. But it does include an increasingly grotesque, gendered aspect, as we noted, that begins with Lear's horror at weeping, because he believes it is unnatural for him, as a man, and therefore must be resisted to the last:

> LEAR
> ... Old fond eyes,
> Beweep this cause again, I'll pluck you out
> And cast you, with the waters that you loose,
> To temper clay. Yea, is 't come to this?
> Ha! Let it be so. I have another daughter
> Who, I am sure, is kind and comfortable.
> When she shall hear this of thee, with her nails
> She'll flay thy wolvish visage. Thou shalt find
> That I'll resume the shape which thou dost think
> I have cast off forever. He exits.
>
> (*KL* 1.4.318-327)

> ... Touch me with noble anger,
> And let not women's weapons, water drops,
> Stain my man's cheeks.—No, you unnatural hags,
> I will have such revenges on you both
> That all the world shall—I will do such things—
> What they are yet I know not, but they shall be
> The terrors of the Earth! You think I'll weep.
> No, I'll not weep.
> I have full cause of weeping, but this heart

> *Storm and tempest.*
> Shall break into a hundred thousand flaws
> Or ere I'll weep.—O Fool, I shall go mad!
>
> (*KL* 2.4.317-327)

As we have seen, part of what makes Lear's speeches so harrowing is how they careen between extremes, and anyone who has seen a decent production probably remembers some of this from the actor playing Lear, alternating between whispering and bellowing, howling incoherently and perfectly enunciating elevated diction, even in the same speech. And the wild alternation in volume or intensity reflects the huge and sudden changes in content. In these two speeches, Lear is clearly understanding, revealing, and contemplating, if not accepting, his abjection, his powerlessness—a powerlessness intrinsic to his nature, but which had been hidden from him his whole life. But then in the next moment, he can reject it utterly, making pathetic threats to "resume the shape which thou dost think/I have cast off forever." This continues in the later speech, with vows to "have such revenges on you both," when he lacks any ability to bring such things to pass.[25] And that is the real realization here. Weeping is not pathetic or even unnatural, for man or woman: cf. the ending, when Lear calls upon all present to cry out and weep, "Howl, howl, howl! O, you are men of stones!/Had I your tongues and eyes, I'd use them so/That heaven's vault should crack" (*King Lear* 5.3.308-310).[26] Vowing revenge when one has no ability to enact such plans—that is pathetic and unnatural. But Lear's prescience at the end of the latter speech is clear and heartbreaking to us: his heart will "break into a hundred thousand flaws" if he continues to repress and deny his nature, and tries to continue to maintain some false nature he has bought into and had reinforced by everyone around him up until now.

Thus we come to the most famous speeches in the play. Removed from society, out in the very dark heart of nature, increasingly divested of clothing, down to four companions who love him truly and selflessly—Lear has been removed from everything that was harming him, everything that was keeping him trapped in a false, artificial world. Everything except himself, of course, and that is what has to be finally broken down out on the heath, to get to (or back to) an authentic human nature that he has been kept from him his whole life. At the very least, and for a start, he can begin by letting go of his shame at weeping. In a driving rainstorm, who would notice, however many tears run down his face? But of course, Lear will not go quietly. Still he must rage at something,[27] and his peculiar knack at this point is to rage at something cosmic and not at his particular situation (even as he clearly still has his own circumstances in mind, with the last line here):

> LEAR
> Blow winds, and crack your cheeks! Rage, blow!
> You cataracts and hurricanoes, spout
> Till you have drenched our steeples, drowned the cocks.
> You sulph'rous and thought-executing fires,
> Vaunt-couriers of oak-cleaving thunderbolts,
> Singe my white head. And thou, all-shaking thunder,
> Strike flat the thick rotundity o' th' world.
> Crack nature's molds, all germens spill at once
> That makes ingrateful man.
>
> (*KL* 3.2.1-11)

Now he no longer calls upon nature to curse those who have harmed him.[28] Now he submits to nature's fury, acknowledges its power over him, revels in his own insignificance. But again, Lear cannot leave it at that (nor would we want him to):

> LEAR
> Rumble thy bellyful! Spit, fire! Spout, rain!
> Nor rain, wind, thunder, fire are my daughters.
> I tax not you, you elements, with unkindness.
> I never gave you kingdom, called you children;
> You owe me no subscription. Then let fall
> Your horrible pleasure. Here I stand your slave,
> A poor, infirm, weak, and despised old man.
> But yet I call you servile ministers,
> That will with two pernicious daughters join
> Your high-engendered battles 'gainst a head
> So old and white as this. O, ho, 'tis foul!
>
> (*KL* 3.2.16-26)

Even by Lear's standards of going from one extreme to another, this speech stands out. He acknowledges nature has no obligation to him; it is impersonal and emotionless ("I tax you not, you elements, with unkindness .... You owe me no subscription"). His own weakness he describes vividly ("A poor, infirm, weak, and despised old man"). But then in the very next line, he is on the attack again, and I think not pathetically, as when he threatened Goneril with violent revenge that he had no ability to actualize. This is not sputtering, impotent rage, but a steady, resigned (if still passionate), "Fuck you," to the universe. The universe is nearly infinite in its power, but therefore null in its fairness, if it goes around picking on sick, weak, little old men. This is a huge improvement for Lear, over his former imaginings that nature was just a giant, cosmic enforcer of his own whims. But resignation is still not quite acceptance, and it is definitely not finding a place of nobility and integrity within such a universe. But those are coming.

Kent of course did not need such extreme education to teach him the frailty and vulnerability of human nature. But he comes upon Lear at this point and shows a better reaction to such a violent, powerful nature:

KENT
Alas, sir, are you here? Things that love night
Love not such nights as these. The wrathful skies
Gallow the very wanderers of the dark
And make them keep their caves. Since I was man,
Such sheets of fire, such bursts of horrid thunder,
Such groans of roaring wind and rain I never
Remember to have heard. Man's nature cannot carry
Th' affliction nor the fear.

(*KL* 3.2.44-51)

Kent has braved the storm, following Lear out of love, and here trying desperately to get him to shelter and safety. "Man's nature cannot carry/Th' affliction nor the fear." Human nature cannot prevail or even survive against the physical nature of the universe—at least, not alone. Kent has overcome "fear" to help Lear, and Gloucester does too. Human nature, which we began this chapter by observing is defined by love, can do more than just resign itself to a physically hostile nature outside. It can do what Kent, the Fool, Gloucester, and Edgar all vividly and repeatedly show in these scenes: love and care for another person in pain and need.

It is no accident, I feel, that the characters who understand the vulnerability and dependence of human nature are either female or of lower social status, servants (or in the case of the Fool, if played by the same actor as Cordelia, some strange combination of these, plus their own special sense of "otherness").[29] Meanwhile, much of the play is about painfully educating Lear (and Gloucester and Edgar)—the old, great, white, male, king, and father—that fulfilling one's human nature is not about asserting authority or power, but about embracing powerlessness, and lovingly helping and serving others. (And of the men who learn this hard lesson in the play, Lear, the one who starts with the most power, is the slowest learner.) It is not that being weak makes one value or admire weakness (contra Nietzsche): it is that holding on to the illusion of power blinds one to the value and inevitability of weakness. This would be another dynamic to observe in Augustine's evaluation of his mother, whom he sees as someone who consistently, throughout her life, practiced virtues in her weakness:

> By persevering in devoted service, and by patience and gentleness, she won over her mother-in-law, who had initially been provoked against her by the whispering of mischievous maids, but now of her own accord informed her son of the servants' meddling tongues that had troubled the domestic peace between herself and her daughter-in-law .... There was another great gift with which you had endowed this bondswoman of yours, in whose womb you created me, O my God, my mercy, and that was the gift of acting as peacemaker whenever she could if friction occurred between souls at variance. She would hear many a bitter accusation from each against the other, of the kind that lumpy, ill-digested discord is wont to belch forth when someone dyspeptic with hatred spews out acid talk to a present friend concerning an absent enemy; but never would she repeat to one anything the other had alleged, except what would be effective in reconciling them. (*Conf.* 9.9.20-21)

Never mind all the patience she had and tears she shed, out of love for her son, or her completely unperturbed attitude toward her own impending death (*Conf.* 9.11.27). Indeed, since an insistence on not weeping is such a hindrance to Lear's self-realization of his nature, it is worth underlining how effusive Monica is with tears throughout *Confessions*:

> She pleaded all the more insistently and with free-flowing tears that he would consent to see me, and discuss matters with me. A little vexed, he answered, "Go away now; but hold on to this: it is inconceivable that he should perish, a son of tears like yours." In her conversations with me later she often recalled that she had taken these words to be an oracle from heaven .... Like all mothers, though far more than most, she loved to have me with her, and she did not know how much joy you were to create for her through my absence. She did not know, and so she wept and wailed, and these cries of pain revealed what there was left of Eve in her, as in anguish she sought the son whom in anguish she had brought to birth. (*Conf.* 3.12.21; 5.8.15)

Augustine also had some male, Stoic reticence about crying (*Conf.* 9.12.29), even as he looks back on the fierce efficacy of tears for Monica, and praises her for the love and faith from which such tears flowed. Spurning tears as unmanly seems another problem shared by the two male protagonists we are considering. Augustine sees himself as having wasted many years in pursuit of worldly honor and influence, goals reserved exclusively for well-born males, while he suffered inwardly and spiritually. But Monica, who had none of the achievements of a supposedly successful male, was in her son's estimation, completely successful as a human being and a follower of Christ. Allowing for the difference in genre (no storms or murders for Augustine), and for the explicitly Christian outlook of Augustine, *Confessions* and *King Lear* are very close in showing this strength in weakness, this spiritual and psychological force that flows in those with little physical strength, social status, or political power. Most if not all of the Beatitudes (Matt. 5:1-12) flow from this view of human nature.

Realizing one's abjection and weakness is not the goal here, though, nor is it even the full truth of human nature. To reconsider Edmund's point about nature and its Darwinian survival of the fittest: if human nature were merely helpless, the species would have long since died out. So as Lear realizes his vulnerability in these scenes, he has to come to some understanding and appreciation of what would make such weakness survivable, as Kent and the Fool seem to know much more instinctively. It is significant and infinitely moving that Lear shows his first signs of this realization in reference to the Fool:

LEAR
My wits begin to turn.—
Come on, my boy. How dost, my boy? Art cold?
I am cold myself.—Where is this straw, my fellow?
The art of our necessities is strange
And can make vile things precious. Come, your hovel.—
Poor Fool and knave, I have one part in my heart
That's sorry yet for thee.

(*KL* 3.2.73-80)

Lear is truly experiencing "the art of our necessities" here in the storm. Things that would have been unthinkable days before (e.g., the king wandering around, unprotected, in a violent thunderstorm) bring in their train other, better, previously unthinkable things (e.g., the king giving preference to the needs and suffering of another).[30] That he first turns with compassion toward the Fool (who reminds us and him of Cordelia) is a natural expansion on the earlier friendly, loving exchanges between them. As noted, the storm is erasing social distinctions (and clothes are coming off, to further that process), and getting Lear to a more natural state, one characterized by both danger and fear, on the one hand, simultaneously with increasing love, care, and compassion, on the other.

As we have seen several times, Lear's trajectory is so moving and believable, in part because it is so halting and uneven, and he begins the next scene again focusing on his own suffering:

LEAR
Thou think'st 'tis much that this contentious storm
Invades us to the skin. So 'tis to thee.
But where the greater malady is fixed,
The lesser is scarce felt. Thou 'dst shun a bear,
But if thy flight lay toward the roaring sea,
Thou 'dst meet the bear i' th' mouth. When the mind's free,
The body's delicate. This tempest in my mind
Doth from my senses take all feeling else
Save what beats there. Filial ingratitude!
Is it not as this mouth should tear this hand

For lifting food to 't? But I will punish home.
No, I will weep no more. In such a night
To shut me out? Pour on. I will endure.
In such a night as this? O Regan, Goneril,
Your old kind father whose frank heart gave all!
O, that way madness lies. Let me shun that;
No more of that.

(*KL* 3.4.8-25)

It has been some time since Lear first began to realize he was not a "kind father," and "frank" seems even more of a stretch,[31] yet here he is again with that kind of self-pity—and worse, self-justification. But with the necessity of unlearning such self-deception growing more and more clear to us, and more urgent to Lear, the last two lines here seem hopeful: to dwell on the wrongs done to him is to remain stuck in his false claims of being "more sinned against than sinning" (*King Lear* 3.2.63). It is a different, worse kind of "madness" than what he has been trying to avoid, which, as painful as it is, is honest and sincere, weeping over the pain he is suffering and the pain he has inflicted. As self-centered as Lear remains (and I think this holds true to the very end of the play), he is slowly, haltingly letting go of lying to himself about his faults and all of his previous life.

He is also following through on his previously shown urges toward sympathy for the plight of others. He again considers the Fool's suffering, but this time it widens into a much more general consideration of human suffering:

LEAR
Prithee, go in thyself. Seek thine own ease.
This tempest will not give me leave to ponder
On things would hurt me more. But I'll go in.—
In, boy; go first.—You houseless poverty—
Nay, get thee in. I'll pray, and then I'll sleep.
Fool exits.
Poor naked wretches, wheresoe'er you are,
That bide the pelting of this pitiless storm,
How shall your houseless heads and unfed sides,
Your looped and windowed raggedness defend you
From seasons such as these? O, I have ta'en
Too little care of this. Take physic, pomp.

> Expose thyself to feel what wretches feel,
> That thou may'st shake the superflux to them
> And show the heavens more just.
>
> (*KL* 3.4.27-41)

The concern for the Fool has become more poignant and touching, "Seek thine own ease." And a moment later, Lear is contemplating all "poor naked wretches" in his kingdom. Depending on the actor's gestures, "I have ta'en/Too little care of this," can either mean Lear feels the weakness of his own body (if he clutches himself in some way as he speaks the line), or that he is feeling some responsibility for the poverty in his kingdom and its concomitant suffering (if he gestures outwardly or at the hovel). I think, given the trajectory of this speech, the latter is more probable (and at age 80 [*King Lear* 4.7.70], in ancient Britain, how much could self-care have improved his hardiness at this point?). By the end of this speech, Lear is expressing exactly the sentiment of the two servants at the end of Act 3, scene 7: "Now heaven help him!" (*King Lear* 3.7.129). People showing kindness attribute it nonetheless to divine or heavenly sources, adding humility to their practiced virtues. Or perhaps, people learning compassion by sharing their goods with one another ("shake the superflux to them"), or more generally, sympathizing with each other by sharing each other's pains and burdens ("Expose thyself to feel what wretches feel"), thereby come to believe in divine, cosmic, or natural justice (or even feel such as the source of their own good and just urges).[32] And if I am right that Lear is expressing regret at his previous neglect here, then he is, as on many other points, trying to undo the injustice his former life and actions have brought about. Human nature here is shown to expand love beyond the particular object in front of one (here, the Fool), to any humans of whose pain one has been made aware. Again, this is not so much a refutation of Edmund's Darwinian urges, but a broader application of them. "The needs of the many outweigh the needs of the few, or the one," is, after all, perfectly compatible with the idea of survival of the fittest, if one is considering the community- or species-wide level, and thinking longer term. But also, it is to think, as Lear does here, of the immediate, of seeing an individual suffering right in front of oneself, in real time, and obeying the instinct to assuage that suffering, and keep on following it, rather than find excuses ("The problem is too big; I can't feed and clothe everyone; there are systemic problems beyond my control," etc.).

Gloucester, newly blinded and in the first waves of despair at his new situation, similarly feels this urge to generosity and alleviating other's suffering, even as his own is beyond anything he could've expected shortly before:

> GLOUCESTER, *giving him money*
> Here, take this purse, thou whom the heavens' plagues
> Have humbled to all strokes. That I am wretched
> Makes thee the happier. Heavens, deal so still:
> Let the superfluous and lust-dieted man,
> That slaves your ordinance, that will not see
> Because he does not feel, feel your power quickly.
> So distribution should undo excess
> And each man have enough.
>
> (*KL* 4.1.73-81)

The description and sentiment are very like Lear's, especially at the end, "So distribution should undo excess/And each man have enough." Gloucester seems even more confused than Lear or the servants, on where the "heavens" fit in this. He had given his grimmest appraisal of them shortly before this speech, "As flies to wanton boys are we to th' gods;/They kill us for their sport" (*King Lear* 4.1.41-42). But here, contemplating the opportunity for sympathizing with and aiding another man, Gloucester softens somewhat and is more ambiguous. On the one hand, he believes the mad beggar before him is in that state because of "heavens' plagues." But in the next lines, he calls upon the "Heavens" to "deal so" with the greedy and unfeeling rich, forcing them to distribute their wealth more fairly. The nature of the heavens seems utterly unknown within the play. But it seems unambiguous on human nature, which is to share in one another's suffering and thereby make it bearable. It seems also in human nature to attribute this urge to some heavenly force(s) outside themselves and which is totally silent on the subject (and on every subject, for that matter).

In this new frame of mind, this more primitive, natural state, even Lear's self-centeredness can lead to new insights. Upon meeting the disguised Edgar, it seems as though Lear's obsession with his own problems will reassert itself, and he will simply subsume this new character into his hallucinations of his own persecution[33]:

> LEAR
> Now all the plagues that in the pendulous air
> Hang fated o'er men's faults light on thy daughters!
>
> KENT
> He hath no daughters, sir.
>
> LEAR
> Death, traitor! Nothing could have subdued nature
> To such a lowness but his unkind daughters.
> Is it the fashion that discarded fathers
> Should have thus little mercy on their flesh?
> Judicious punishment! 'Twas this flesh begot
> Those pelican daughters.
>
> (*KL* 3.4.73-81)

But then, as with unexpectedly turning to let the Fool seek shelter before himself, there is something in Lear's "wits begin[ning] to turn" that gives him more insight than he had when he was warm and dry and safe. Though he imagines and insists that Edgar's problems are just like his own (because he's so focused on those), he begins to consider Edgar in a more detached way, an other-directed and not self-absorbed way, not including any fantasies of his imaginary "pelican daughters":

> LEAR
> Thou wert better in a grave than to answer with
> thy uncovered body this extremity of the skies.—Is
> man no more than this? Consider him well.—Thou
> ow'st the worm no silk, the beast no hide, the sheep
> no wool, the cat no perfume. Ha, here's three on 's
> are sophisticated. Thou art the thing itself; unaccommodated
> man is no more but such a poor, bare,
> forked animal as thou art. Off, off, you lendings!
> Come, unbutton here. *Tearing off his clothes.*
>
> (*KL* 3.4.108-115)

It seems one of Lear's grimmest lines, this contemplation of "a poor, bare, forked animal." And at some level, at the confession of complete vulnerability, it is frank and resigned, but no longer in the angry way noted above, railing at the storm, but bemused and pitying of this frail creature, surviving nonetheless in the midst of the storm. Lear even seems almost to be admiring this creature, who is living as free and "unaccommodated" (or "unburdened"?) as Lear wishes to be. Look at the things the "forked animal" does without—clothes and perfume, the marks of falsifying court life that Lear keeps returning to (and which Edgar encouraged in his preceding speech of feigned madness), and of which he ends this speech divesting himself, again.[34] But even more than admiration, finally, there seems almost love for this creature like himself, because it (and himself) are now known for what they truly are, and the resemblance leads to compassion and love.[35]

With so many characters in this play behaving unnaturally, by the definition we have formed, but inhabiting a universe where there seems to be no divine or heavenly beings punishing or avenging such behavior, we should consider what is their fate. On this Shakespeare seems to hold out three possible outcomes. The unnatural person may be killed by a person following more natural urges. This is the fate of Oswald and Cornwall, facilitated by both of them underestimating the strength of those behaving more naturally than they are. And in both their cases, blinded by social class, they think a "mere" peasant could not harm them—another indication, if one were needed, that social status and the trappings of it are depicted as distinctly unnatural in the play.

Such is the fate of the secondary villains (the more typical term for the unnatural people in the play). Working our way up to primary villains, Goneril and Regan destroy themselves (or Goneril kills both of them). Albany had predicted this much earlier in the play:

ALBANY
… O Goneril
You are not worth the dust which the rude wind
Blows in your face. I fear your disposition.
That nature which contemns its origin
Cannot be bordered certain in itself.
She that herself will sliver and disbranch

From her material sap perforce must wither
And come to deadly use.

(*KL* 4.2.38-45)

To be unnatural is to have a nature even more conflicted with itself than regular human nature, which we defined as containing deep dissatisfactions with its own urges and desires. But whereas the conflicts of regular human nature drive it to seek a higher, supernatural Being (God), the conflict in these unnatural characters "contemns its origin" and then turns even on itself, causing itself to "sliver and disbranch" and then "wither," literally tearing itself apart. One production I saw did this so simply and brilliantly by having the curtain rise after the intermission on a set that had all the props we had already seen—tables, flags, chairs, throne—but all shattered into smithereens and scattered all over the stage, sometimes an item by itself, sometimes a little pile of them. The audience gasped audibly but then it became clear that the evil characters didn't notice anything was wrong—because to them it wasn't. They moved about the set just as they had before, or with considerably more ease and impunity, Goneril and Edmund even beginning Act 4, scene 2, by fucking behind a trash heap.[36] That the world is devolving into chaos perfectly suits them, as Albany goes on to observe:

ALBANY
Wisdom and goodness to the vile seem vile.
Filths savor but themselves. What have you done?
Tigers, not daughters, what have you performed?
A father, and a gracious agèd man,
Whose reverence even the head-lugged bear would lick,
Most barbarous, most degenerate, have you madded.
Could my good brother suffer you to do it?
A man, a prince, by him so benefited!
If that the heavens do not their visible spirits
Send quickly down to tame these vile offenses,
It will come:
Humanity must perforce prey on itself,
Like monsters of the deep.

(*KL* 4.2.47-61)

"Filths savor but themselves," makes it sound as though living in a junkyard rather than a palace is just a matter of taste, but Albany claims it is more self-destructive than that: "Humanity must perforce prey on itself,/Like monsters of the deep." The more unnatural behavior of Goneril and Regan (Oswald and Cornwall only harm their king and other unrelated people, not their actual father), is so diseased it doesn't take a good person standing up to it, to bring about its end; it destroys itself. And here again, the more pious character, Albany, holds out some hope this reckoning and extermination might come from a divine or heavenly source ("If that the heavens do not their visible spirits/Send quickly down to tame these vile offenses"), though even he admits this may not happen, but the unnaturalness is too great to survive, even absent divine punishment.

The villain who sets all this in motion (Goneril and Regan are opportunists, after all, and do not come on stage with a plan to bring about all this destruction) is Edmund, and just as he has the most interesting and complex ideas about nature, his unnatural dealings have the most interesting and ambiguous end:

EDMUND, *to Edgar*
What you have charged me with, that have I done,
And more, much more. The time will bring it out.
'Tis past, and so am I. But what art thou
That hast this fortune on me? If thou 'rt noble,
I do forgive thee.

EDGAR
Let's exchange charity.
I am no less in blood than thou art, Edmund;
If more, the more th' hast wronged me.
My name is Edgar and thy father's son.
The gods are just, and of our pleasant vices
Make instruments to plague us.
The dark and vicious place where thee he got
Cost him his eyes.

EDMUND
Th' hast spoken right. 'Tis true.
The wheel is come full circle; I am here.

(*KL* 5.3.195-209)

Only Edmund has even the possibility of "charity," of forgiving and being forgiven (and this is actualized because Edgar has learned compassion).[37] Before he dies, he goes even further than being reconciled to Edgar. He also tries to stop further evil: "Some good I mean to do/Despite of mine own nature" (*King Lear* 5.3.291-292). From our examination, this would not be "despite" his nature, any more than Lear's weeping and raving and disrobing are against his real nature. Rather, Lear's acts of self-abnegation and Edmund's act of mercy are trying to get at real, human nature, which is characterized by love and compassion. And here again, mere human agency doesn't quite satisfy the characters. Edgar picks this moment to utter the most devout line in the whole play, "The gods are just." And interestingly, not because the gods have helped him kill Edmund, but because Edmund is a product of Gloucester's own "pleasant vices" and therefore Gloucester's suffering was just (though it still elicited heroic compassion from his estranged son). It's Edmund who connects this to some sense of justice in his own death, by finally accepting the idea of the wheel of fortune that he had previously rejected, but attaching it here to Edgar's lines, that their father's sins affected everyone, but Edmund played a willing role and therefore suffers for his own sinful, unnatural behavior ("If more, the more th' hast wronged me"). Everyone in the Gloucester family at least is where they belong, based on their actions. And mercifully, everyone in that family has forgiven each other, a peace denied the Lear family.

After this lengthy tour of these two masterpieces, we can formulate some unified theory of human nature from the two of them together. Human nature is to love other humans in some relationship(s) of trust and dependence, what one scholar movingly and pithily called "a network of mutual need."[38] This trusting and depending is the source of human survival and thriving, or simply a given of human existence,[39] but it is also confused and conflicted, because it involves giving up some freedom and autonomy. Sin, error, and self-destruction come in when one tries to get the benefits and support of love without giving up one's autonomy or contributing to the relationship—then one is some species of abuser or deceiver.[40] This loving human nature is reliant on and a part of nature more generally, of the physical, natural world. This world we humans also trust to be reliable, thinking (rightly) that there are mathematical, physical, chemical, biological laws governing it. But we often wrongly further assume that its laws are there for our benefit or comfort, or that it is fully understandable and tractable to human needs, exploitable to human demands. Nature and natural laws are knowable by us (to some extent), but do not respect our needs or desires. We must respect and work around the laws of nature, shape and limit our expectations and desires to them, not them to our needs. And this is one point where it does not matter if we substitute "God" for "nature"—even if we believe God loves us, God does so in such a way that it might include us being covered in boils, or slaughtered by bandits, or killed in a storm or earthquake or meteor strike, as unpleasant as any of those would be for us, and as incompatible with any standard idea we might have of being loved. Writing this in the midst of a global pandemic, while still believing God loves me and all people, and while some of my fellows insist it is their right to gather in large groups and not wear masks, those words seem more relevant to me than if I'd penned them a year ago. Rather, the sheer magnitude and implacability of nature (or God, if you will), means the only appropriate response is to be confirmed in our own weakness and dependence on it, and go back to the urges of our own human nature. In a universe so enormous and so unconcerned with our safety or enjoyment, loving and caring for others is reaffirmed, as the only way we could survive or thrive, individually or as a group.

All of this loving and caring finds expression sometimes in speech since we are also speaking animals and cannot rely solely on deeds and nonverbal communication. Whether it is wooing or convincing or praising or even cursing, we cannot hold our ideas and feelings inside, and we feel compelled to give them voice. But here again there is ambivalence or frustration: we cannot help but speak, but we cannot help but feel and know speech is not enough, that it is necessary and inevitable, but also inadequate. This is even more the case for one special kind of speaking—expressing rational thought or argument. If Cordelia rightly objects that her "love's/More ponderous than my tongue," and that she "cannot heave/My heart into my mouth" (*King Lear* 1.1.86-87, 100-101), she would be equally justified in saying her tongue and mouth cannot properly and fully articulate what is in her head, any more than they can what is in her heart.[41] She might also note what she herself struggles with, that her head and heart do not properly coordinate their messages, both of them speaking in quite different idioms, each perhaps right in its own sphere and as far as it goes, but together confusing each other, and those to whom they try to communicate.[42] We turn now to those special communication problems raised by trying to put reason into words, and the often observed disconnect or conflict between thought and feelings, reason and passion, head and heart.

Notes

1 Though Miles, *Augustine and the Fundamentalist's Daughter*, 20, is right to remind us that while Augustine's diagnosis is grim, it is sympathetic and not condemnatory of the patient/sinner/infant: "Clearly, Augustine did not regard infancy with rose-colored glasses. It is important, and only fair, however, to notice that although 'sin' is a judgmental word in our contemporary usage, Augustine insisted that the appropriate attitude toward sin is not condemnation but sympathy."

2 Cf. Vaught, *Journey toward God in Augustine's* Confessions. *Books I–VI*, 32: "In its futile efforts to find the gratification it seeks, the frustration of its will externalizes itself; and its consequent outbursts point to a radical discontinuity that disrupts the positive community out of which it emerges .... The infant's struggles to express its desires reflect a fundamental opposition between positive and negative elements in its nature, and it is out of this internal conflict that a negative community of fallen individuals emerges. In this case, the finitude of innocence becomes the fallenness of alienation, and this alienation manifests itself, not only in relation to others, but also in relation to ourselves."

3 This of course goes for most sinful behavior, as noted by Miles, *Augustine and the Fundamentalist's Daughter*, 43: "Augustine was careful to say that it was not that anything he attempted to clutch was unworthy in itself; it was the anxious grasping itself that was the problem." Though speaking of Lear, Morris, *Shakespeare's God*, 360, describes the exact same dynamic and locus of sin: "He finds, as they do, that these external goods not only cannot make a man better, but that their goodness depends entirely upon the manner in which they are desired, and exists only in so far as they are not made part of the soul of him who covets them."

4 And even shown in non-glaring facial expressions, as observed by Miles, *Augustine and the Fundamentalist's Daughter*, 16: "Maxine Sheets-Johnstone argues that the infant's smile is not only intentional, but it is also 'an initiatory act', not a response."

5 Cf. Bloom, *Shakespeare*, 509: "This is so horrible as to court grotesque comedy, if anyone other than Lear shouted it forth."

6 Cf. McFarland, "Image of the Family," 105: "Or to summon a modern reference to counterbalance Laing, the family image in *King Lear* is what in Christopher Lasch's rubric is termed 'haven in a heartless world'."

7 Cf. McFarland, "Image of the Family," 95: "The situation in *King Lear* involves a different model of experience, an image of family life that is neither flamboyant nor unique. On the contrary, it is in significant respects almost commonplace. Lear's pain and outrage are larger versions of the pain and outrage that almost all parents at some point and to some degree experience because of their offspring."

8 Cf. Bloom, *Shakespeare*, 492: "Johnson speaks of sexual love, rather than familial love, a distinction Shakespeare taught Freud partly to avoid .... Lear's excessive love transcends even his attachment to Cordelia; it comprehends the Fool and others. The worship of Lear by Kent, Gloucester, Albany, and most of all his godson Edgar is directed not only at the great image of authority but at the central emblem of familial love, or patriarchal love (if you would have it so)."

9 Also very likely an allusion to his love as Christ-like. See Janet Adelman, "Introduction," in *Twentieth Century Interpretations of King Lear: A Collection of Critical Essays*, edited by Janet Adelman (Englewood Cliffs, NJ: Prentice-Hall, 1978), 1–21, esp. 4: "'O thou side-piercing sight!' (IV.iv.85) he cries, in words that suggest a Christ-like compassion—literally *feeling with*—for the sorrows of mankind, and of the particular men in front of him" (emphasis in original).

10 And cf. the incredible and beautiful associations of Cordelia as mother, made by McFarland, "Image of the Family," 110: "Cordelia, hovering over his bed, is, in awesome psycho-dramatic recapitulation, the eternal mother brooding over the infant's crib."

11 Cf. the provocative speculations about the Fool, by Bloom, *Shakespeare*, 495: "Lear loves him and treats him as a child, but the Fool is of no determinate age, though clearly he will not grow up. Is he altogether human, or a sprite or changeling? His utterances differ sharply from those of any court fool in Shakespeare; he alone seems to belong to an occult world."

12 Cf. L. C. Knights, "On the Fool," in *Twentieth Century Interpretations of King Lear: A Collection of Critical Essays*, edited by Janet Adelman (Englewood Cliffs, NJ: Prentice-Hall, 1978), 122–3, esp. 123: "It is through him [the Fool], therefore, that we come to see more clearly the sharp distinction between those whose wisdom is purely for themselves and those foolish ones—Kent, Gloucester, Cordelia, and the Fool himself—who recklessly take their stand on loyalties and sympathies that are quite outside the scope of any prudential calculus."

13 This observation from John-Paul Spiro of Villanova University, gratefully acknowledged here.
14 Cf. Alfred Harbage, "Introduction," to *King Lear*; The Pelican Shakespeare (New York: Penguin Books, 1958 [rev. ed. 1970]) 19: "To imitate the dominant animal imagery of the style, Cornwall is less repellent than Goneril and Regan only as the mad bull is less repellent than the hyena, they less repellent than Oswald only as the hyena is less repellent than the jackal. To the latter he failed to give even that engaging touch of the ludicrous usually reserved for assistant villains."
15 Cf. Miles, *Augustine and the Fundamentalist's Daughter*, 219: "Augustine taught that human loves do not compete with love of God, but rather *participate* in God-is-love .... Augustine claims that a person loves God *by* loving others" (emphasis in original).
16 Cf. McFarland, "Image of the Family," 113: "Edmund's position as bastard both threatens the normative structure of the family and reveals him as the initial legatee of family pain."
17 Cf. McFarland, "Image of the Family," 115: "The bastard stands outside the haven represented by the family, apparently fully accepting the situation as laid down by his inattentive and carelessly joking father. But when we see the bastard alone, we understand how little those grouped hierarchies actually answer to the structure of human need."
18 Again, they needn't be killed, necessarily, though there's also nothing in Edmund or his concept of love, that would rule that out, should it become advantageous to do so.
19 Cf. Bloom, *Shakespeare*, 496: "Lear's madness is much debated: his revulsion from Goneril and Regan becomes an involuntary horror of female sexuality."
20 This blasphemous setting himself up as God continues as his cursing of Goneril and Regan intensifies, and is noted by Boitani, *Gospel according to Shakespeare*, 28: "Lear alternates, as he had done shortly before, between the Passion and the *patientia* of Job and Christ, on the one hand, and the most unbridled fury that Yahweh shows against his enemies in the Hebrew Bible .... He is also a disturbing and perverse image of Yahweh, He who commands tempests."
21 Cf. Hackett, "'And Thou, all-Shaking Thunder'," "At the beginning of the play (I.1, I.4), Lear is self-assured that his kingship serves, one could say, as the keystone, the bridge, between the order of nature and human culture, guaranteeing justice—or rather, to express it more modestly, that justice is on his side. Yet the unfolding of the play dramatically betrays this. The journey through madness and back again, through divesture of throne, and even clothing (in

imitation of Poor Tom), naked in the wild and storm, without a home, and back, being covered by the Fool, and taking shelter in a hovel, eventually given new clothes, descent into the storm and out gives evidence of a justice that involves both nature and convention, and that is not a human possession: it afflicts and rescues; but it is not fully comprehensible. It certainly does not play in any privileged one's favor."

22 On the family resemblance (even including Edmund), see S. L. Goldberg, "On Edgar's Character," in *Twentieth Century Interpretations of King Lear: A Collection of Critical Essays*, edited by Janet Adelman (Englewood Cliffs, NJ: Prentice-Hall, 1978), 114–16, esp. 115: "Edgar ... is a true member of the Gloucester family, all of whom in one way or another seem insecure and anxious about themselves, and whose characteristic psychic style is defensive beside the bolder, more challenging, self-confidently active style characteristic of the Lear family."

23 Cf. Vaught, *Journey toward God in Augustine's* Confessions. *Books I–VI*, 81: "Images (*phantasiae*) are products of the reproductive imagination and correspond more or less adequately to reality, while fantasies (*phantasmae*) are products of the productive imagination that do not correspond to anything at all. It is images of the second kind, and the radical deception to which they lead, that Augustine accuses the Manichaeans of trying to foist on him."

24 Cf. Boitani, *Gospel according to Shakespeare*, 4: "In particular, the feeling of the presence of divinity is born initially, in Shakespeare's characters, from pain, from suffering that which is obscure and tragic, and from the experience of death." Also Rice, "Empathic Edgar," 52: "But despite man's vulnerability, Gloucester's vision of man as a worm is contradicted by Edgar's compassionate presence."

25 Cf. McFarland, "Image of the Family," 99: "The protagonistic function is thus dispersed, and the dispersal is both welcome and in a sense necessary because of the unattractiveness of age .... [this] gives him immense tragic authenticity and the play immense leverage at the tragic intersection of being and nonbeing, by the same token, his standing at the verge of nature's confine makes it difficult for us to identify with him. For an aged man is but a paltry thing."

26 On the emotions in his final speeches, see Edelstein, *Thinking Shakespeare*, 18: "Lear speaks as he does because of his infinite pain, because of his powerlessness before a random universe, because of his despair at the wretched and unjust fact that those we love must one day die."

27 Cf. Bloom, *Shakespeare*, 510: "Perpetually outraged, except for the brief idyll of his reconciliation with Cordelia, Lear appeals

primordially to the universal outrage of all those acutely conscious of their own mortality. Resentment, justified or not, is part of social psychology; the sense of being outraged need have no social component whatsoever. We die as individuals, however generous or benighted our public sympathies may be. Lear's peculiar intimacy with us, as our dead father, partly depends on this shared sense of outrage." See also Ruth Nevo, "On Lear and Job," in *Twentieth Century Interpretations of King Lear: A Collection of Critical Essays*, edited by Janet Adelman (Englewood Cliffs, NJ: Prentice-Hall, 1978), 120–2, esp. 121: "Lear, raging in the storm, is no hero of renunciation but of an enormous expostulation; 'raging, ravening and uprooting into the desolation of reality'" (quoting from Harbage).

28 Though cf. Boitani, *Gospel according to Shakespeare*, 29, who makes this of a piece with Lear's earlier cursing and setting himself up as God: "But how different is Lear from Job's God! God, thundering from the vortex of his tempest, evokes his own Creation. Lear, on the other hand, from his hurricane wants destruction (perhaps even of Christian civilization, with its steeples and the cocks surmounting them), a second Flood, the flattening out of Earth, the return of being—of Nature—to nothingness."

29 On the Fool's special insight into nature, see Knights, "On the Fool," 122–3: "The world picture he creates is of small creatures in a world too big—and in its human aspects, too bad—to be anything but bewildering. His sharply realistic, commonplace instances—like Tom's mad talk, though with a different tone—insist on the alien aspect of Nature, and on all that detracts from man's sense of his own dignity—corns, chilblains, lice, and the mere pricking of sexual desire."

30 Cf. Morris, *Shakespeare's God*, 363: "For though he has hardened his own heart to grievous effect, Lear knows he was moved at least as much by horror at apparent unnaturalness as by unkindness of his own. He can claim to be a man more sinned against than sinning; and in the 'more than kingly dignity' of his concern for the shivering wretch at his side there is testimony to the kindness of a nature truly royal."

31 Though, as above, perhaps it is part of what Bloom, *Shakespeare*, 509, sees as Lear's "wholeheartedness."

32 Thus Boitani, *Gospel according to Shakespeare*, 30: "Lear then remembers the poor and understands that he has to make himself like them; as he becomes capable of pity and charity, he understands the possibility of the existence of divine justice."

33 As noted by Williams, *Tragic Imagination*, 38: "But the interruption of the discovery of Poor Tom seems to push him back into his obsessional talk of ingratitude."

34 Cf. Morris, *Shakespeare's God*, 363–4: "It is 'a means of liberating for full flight an imagination that was hampered before', and thus renders possible that clearing away of the untruth of appearances that enables the soul to attain to higher awareness within the external order and its own being .... He may not see in Tom the nature of humanity corrupted by its sin; but eagerly putting off with his clothes the old beliefs of his grandeur if not of his righteousness, he seeks, arrayed in the new truth manifested in his ragged 'philosopher', to become, like his mentor, 'a thing of external, instinctive life'." Going beyond clothing to independence more broadly, cf. Williams, *Tragic Imagination*, 37: "The key word is 'ow'st': Poor Tom is not in debt to anyone or anything. This is what it is to be an independent human agent. And the audience is prompted to think back on the whole trajectory of Lear's journey to this point." And most optimistically of all, see Rice, "Empathic Edgar," 59: "When the divisions are erased and the individual has been exposed as the 'poor thing' Lear discovers him to be—that is the portal of the Kingdom of God." In similarly, explicitly Christian terms, see Basney, "Is a Christian Perspective on Shakespeare Productive and/or Necessary?" 33: "The implication of this is clear: it is when the cultural orders that allow love to be expressed but that have been violated break down that grace suddenly becomes available."

35 Thus Boitani, *Gospel according to Shakespeare*, 30: "Lear turns to poor Tom with words that reveal how he is now reaching out towards the essence itself of humankind. This is charity, yes, but also ultimate knowledge."

36 Thus, without the explicitly sexual content, McFarland, "Image of the Family," 113: "He [Edmund] thereby becomes the leader, as it were, the first in line, of those who descend toward the disintegrative bleakness of the world of storm and night."

37 Cf. Rice, "Empathic Edgar," 57: "Since he has already shown us that the feeling behind words is more important than any concept of absolute truth, it is consistent for Edgar to sympathize with Edmund after he has mortally wounded him." Also Murphy, *Darkness and Devils*, 214: "And further, while I would not insist on an unequivocally Christian sense to be given to Edmund's final language, I would insist that it does not attack or disparage repentance and at least here is a drama of redemption."

38 See Williams, *Tragic Imagination*, 38: "In place of a network of mutual need, what characterizes human society is the calculation of purchasing power. The economic language of the opening scene comes back with a vengeance: there is only the market—not even the partially disguised, collusive 'market' of comforting words that

is invoked in the opening scene, but the naked buying of safety and well-being and public immunity, with nothing for those who lack purchasing power." Similarly, see Kenneth Muir, "On Christian Values," in *Twentieth Century Interpretations of King Lear: A Collection of Critical Essays*, edited by Janet Adelman (Englewood Cliffs, NJ: Prentice-Hall, 1978), 120: "In a world of lust, cruelty and greed, with extremes of wealth and poverty, man reduced to his essentials needs not wealth, nor power, nor even physical freedom, but rather patience, stoical fortitude, and love; needs, perhaps, above all, mutual forgiveness, the exchange of charity, and those sacrifices on which the gods, if there are any gods, throw incense."

39 Cf. Williams, *Tragic Imagination*, 40: "The interdependence of human love is indeed 'immeasurable', but not in the sense that Lear imagines; the identity of each and all is grounded in an indebtedness that cannot be quantified, since it is simply a function of our being located where we are in a world, with the actual interdependence we have .... The debt under which we all lie is what belongs to a common condition in which we cannot live without recognizing what we need from the human other, in family or in society."

40 Cf. Williams, *Tragic Imagination*, 40: "The person who fantasizes *either* that he or she can make unlimited demands as a matter of right *or* (which comes, Shakespeare suggests, to the same thing) that there can be a human life free of 'owing' is destined for tragic catastrophe" (emphasis in original). Cf. also the divisions of the lower circles of Hell in Dante's *Inferno*, into those sinners guilty of violence, and those who practiced fraud. Throughout this analysis, I have held myself back from bringing Dante into the discussion more, but on this point his very different, mythical world fits Augustine's and Shakespeare's.

41 Though cf. the fascinating discussion of non-intellectual thought given by Edelstein, *Thinking Shakespeare*, 17: "But thought in Shakespeare frequently comes from a *non-intellectual* place. Hamlet refers to his constant need to 'unpack my heart with words' .... And because the thoughts behind Shakespeare's text frequently transcend intellect, the actor must open his own intellectual process to the possibility that his creative expression may take him beyond reason" (emphasis in original).

42 Cf. the discussion of how feeling, thinking, and speaking relate given by Edelstein, *Thinking Shakespeare*, 19: "Nonetheless, this book is called *Thinking Shakespeare*, rather than *Feeling Shakespeare*, because *thinking* is the crux. Thinking is the beginning of a process that leads to speaking, and then to feeling. That's a truth that every one of Shakespeare's characters knows" (emphasis and titles in

original). See also his later discussion of wit and heart—Edelstein, *Thinking Shakespeare*, 308–9: "Michael Langham, the great Shakespearean director .... said (with an expert use of antithesis), 'You act Chekhov with your heart. But you act Shakespeare with your wit' .... But it does mean that in Shakespeare, *wit comes first*. In classical material, feeling must be balanced with the understanding that *what the character says* is as important as what he feels.
In classical acting, the way in which a character expresses his thoughts points to the nature, texture, and emotions of the thoughts themselves."

4

The Problem of Reason

The problem of reason is implicit throughout *Confessions*. We have touched on it when thinking of the scene in the garden in Book Eight, and in the discussion of "some books by the Platonists" (*Conf.* 7.9.13), and how those books convinced Augustine of something, yet that did not result in the desired or expected change for which he had been looking and longing, hoping and planning, his mother weeping, and him praying.[1] The problem is simply that we (hopefully) try to make reason a part of most every decision we make, but something more is needed. Just seeing the logic or reason in a situation is not sufficient to convince us to act. Although this is part of the overall flow of *Confessions*, Augustine presents it at its most outrageous and frustrating, in a famous passage we haven't examined yet:

> But now self-abhorrence possessed me, all the harsher as my heart went out more ardently to those young men, and I heard of the blessed impulsiveness with which they had without reserve handed themselves over to you for healing. By contrast with them I felt myself loathsome, remembering how many of my years—twelve, perhaps—had gone to waste, and I with them, since my nineteenth year when I was aroused to pursue wisdom by the reading of Cicero's *Hortensius*. I had been putting off the moment when by spurning earthly happiness I would clear space in my life to search for wisdom; yet even to seek it, let alone find it, would have been more rewarding than discovery of treasure or possession of all this world's kingdoms, or having every bodily pleasure at my beck and call. I had been extremely

> miserable in adolescence, miserable from its very onset, and as I prayed to you for the gift of chastity I had even pleaded, "Grant me chastity and self-control, but please not yet." I was afraid that you might hear me immediately and heal me forthwith of the morbid lust which I was more anxious to satisfy than to snuff out. (*Conf.* 8.7.17)

Augustine claims his mind had been convinced by that point, enough that he knows what he wants and asks God for it. His mind is made up. But not really: "chastity ... but." As with the pear tree, it's a scene in *Confessions* that seems utterly believable. We all have reviewed the reasons for a decision, subjected it to examination by our reason, convinced ourselves of the right course of action, and yet felt ourselves paralyzed to act, to actually make the decision. But as with the pear tree, is it as big a deal as Augustine makes it out to be? And a lot more relies on this scene than the pear tree, as it really has been what has driven all the events and decisions and actions of the first eight books of *Confessions*, this decision that needs to be made, for which the narrator has lined everything up, to make it seem as though the decision has to be made a certain way, there's no other choice, really; but still the choice just sits there before the great decider, undecided.

And Augustine is here his usual, rhetorically unrestrained self. A normal person would look back on a decision, even a very important one, that he or she had found difficult to decide, and shrug it off as just a particularly difficult one, one that was so evenly balanced between pro and con that it didn't admit of a quick or easy choice. But not our Augustine. He looks upon himself with "self-abhorrence." He finds himself "loathsome" and "miserable," in the grips of "morbid lust." He believes his life has "gone to waste." Without encouraging any reader to feel such self-loathing as we see here, I will say that I think Augustine is on to something here, something more even than he was with angry babies and dissipated youths. Because here he is an adult, and the feelings and the conflict cannot be put off on not knowing better, as they can be with babies (where really, it would be a matter of not knowing anything at all), or teens (excusably, for most of us, because they are overwhelmed by hormones and peer pressure). Augustine describes here a scene from adulthood that we have to admit is within our experience—that even when we know better, we look right at the decision to do good, knowing the right decision, and either choose bad (choosing against our choice), or choose not to choose (which is also bad). The only ideal situation for Augustine would be a "blessed impulsiveness with which they had without reserve handed themselves over to you for healing," but that's not something we can choose—it's a grace bestowed on some people when the time is right (i.e., when God decides to). So hyperbole aside, Augustine is making us uncomfortable not because what he's saying is absurd, but because it seems all too plausible and frequent, and insidiously corrosive of our happiness and fulfillment.

So let us avoid the moralizing judgment here of loathing and abhorring, but consider that Augustine has made an accurate and dire diagnosis of how our minds work, or how they are fundamentally broken. Even in adulthood, with all reason being applied to all the causes and effects we can research, something in our nature (and this further unpacks the problems we saw in our previous chapter), is so conflicted that we cannot even say, "I want that," because the "I" there is not some unity, and therefore the "that" cannot be chosen, or even narrowed down to just one "that." So internally we are such a mess, we would be reduced to just an incoherent, primal scream of, "WANT!"—a verb without subject or object. As I think about this now, it is frighteningly close to the self-defeating, unnatural urges we saw in Goneril in the previous chapter (and I've seen productions where Goneril and Regan shriek or howl in later scenes and now I wonder if it's not just following up on the play's constant use of animal imagery, but is getting at some of this fractured, internal incoherence). And now it's not some monstrous patricidal and sororicidal urges that devolve into self-destruction. It's a much more everyday experience that I can't do what I want because I don't know what I want, and explaining it to myself (or to others, or having them explain it to me) seems to offer little help in the decision.

To focus on the futility of explaining oneself: in some ways that is a great undermining of the whole project of *Confessions*. For himself or other humans, Augustine cannot explain himself, because his observation later equally applies throughout his narrative of his life: "I have become an enigma to myself" (*Conf.* 10.33.50). And to try to explain himself to God is both impossible (because Augustine couldn't formulate such an explanation) and unnecessary, because God already completely knows him (and everyone else):

> Accept the sacrifice of my confessions, offered to you by the power of this tongue of mine which you have fashioned and aroused to confess to your name; bring healing to my bones and let them exclaim, *Lord, who is like you?* A person who confesses to you is not informing you about what goes on within him, for a closed heart does not shut you out, nor is your hand pushed away by human obduracy; you melt it when you choose, whether by showing mercy or by enforcing your claim, and from your fiery heat no one can hide. (*Conf.* 5.1.1)

But if not "informing," still "confessing," and throughout in the sense of praise. It is possible to tell one's life as confession, praise of the God who gave the life. But any human life, or the decisions that made up that life, is finally mysterious, unexplainable, not the sum total of explainable phenomena that went into it. Again, back to my Introduction: where would one even begin such an explanation, without going all the way back to Adam and Eve (or Lucy or whatever primal ancestor science would have me look to), back to things and people that are beyond my knowing or explaining, in some crazy attempt to explain myself, whom I do know, but can't explain?

But as I began this chapter: we try to make reason part of our lives and decisions. To claim more: it *is* a necessary part of our lives and decisions, but not sufficient. Augustine could have just said, "One day I heard some kids playing and suddenly I decided to devote my life to God and live in celibacy," and it would have been accurate, as far as it went, but it wouldn't go far, for Augustine or us. The explanations or reasons that neither Augustine nor we find sufficient, finally, still need to be stated and examined, or any life would just look like a series of arbitrary decisions—or maybe worse, the results of chance or fortune, as we saw when looking at astrology in both texts. And that also would be inaccurate, and not something for which to praise God, because God did not make this world to be arbitrary or fated, but to be guided by God's grace and our free wills cooperating with that grace. God is only praised rightly for the providential guiding of our lives, including all the books and people and illnesses and voyages which we experienced, to which we applied our reason (and other faculties), and which then became part of our decisions and lives.

Observing that explaining oneself is both necessary and futile, ultimately makes a great deal more sense of the latter part of Cordelia's response in the opening scene, because explain herself is exactly what she attempts, with disastrous futility:

> CORDELIA
> ... Good my lord,
> You have begot me, bred me, loved me.
> I return those duties back as are right fit:
> Obey you, love you, and most honor you.
> Why have my sisters husbands if they say
> They love you all? Haply, when I shall wed,
> That lord whose hand must take my plight shall carry
> Half my love with him, half my care and duty.
> Sure I shall never marry like my sisters,
> To love my father all.
>
> LEAR
> But goes thy heart with this?
>
> CORDELIA
> Ay, my good lord.
>
> LEAR
> So young and so untender?
>
> CORDELIA
> So young, my lord, and true.
>
> (*KL* 1.1.105-119)

How different than her more emotional asides just previous to this speech, such as, "I am sure my love's/More ponderous than my tongue" (*King Lear* 1.1.86-87). To say her love exceeds speech is both true and is more like what her father seems to expect. (It is exactly what Goneril said, as we saw in our chapter on language, and to which Lear had no objection.) But it is not, I think, reasonable, or it denies the reasonability of love and just proclaims it an ineffable mystery. This speech here attempts to reason and justify love and that is why it veers off in a direction that is both hurtful and inaccurate.

Cordelia instead starts here with the claim that love is based on "duties" and is therefore "right." She evacuates it of any emotional content (or ignores such content): you love people because you have to, based on connections you did not choose. But this is not true, ultimately. She's standing before her two sisters who clearly love neither their father, nor her, nor their husbands, nor one another—nor even themselves, ultimately. So to love according to a bond seems much more deliberate and less automatic than Cordelia here makes it out to be. To put it in grossly practical terms: I am the first to admit that industries have profited hugely by convincing us we have to buy cards, flowers, chocolate, stuffed animals, even diamonds, to show our love, and such display has reached ridiculous extremes. But they have succeeded, I would say, because some outward sign *is* necessary—they just have seized and capitalized on an urge we all have and exaggerated it for their own profit. To return to the topic of this chapter: Cordelia here rightly describes the reasonable basis of filial love—that the parent has kept the child alive and helped it to thrive, when it would have been easier (in some ways) not to. But the reasonable part of love is not the whole story, nor the best or biggest part of it, even.

This first part of Cordelia's answer follows on the end of her previous speech: "I love your majesty/According to my bond, no more nor less" (*King Lear* 1.1.101-102). But Cordelia follows it up with logic that is even more disastrous: "Why have my sisters husbands if they say/They love you all?" (*King Lear* 1.1.109-110). She goes on the attack, assailing the obvious illogic of what her sisters said. They had both claimed (and with Regan, in clearly incestuous terms) not just that they love their father more than their husbands (or anyone or anything else), but that they love him instead of them (or anyone or anything else): ergo, they do not love their husbands, so why are they married to them? Logical, yes, but Lear asked for a display, not a debate, so such proof or refutation was simply and catastrophically unnecessary. Lear had already listened to Goneril and Regan, and "rewarded" them. If anything, he had arranged this whole scene with the assumption they would say insincere, empty words, and giving them parts of the kingdom was just to placate them. The only words of love Lear showed any interest in or reaction to, would be Cordelia's. So to attack her sisters' words, rather than give her own, is again to privilege logic (since what they said was illogical in the way Cordelia points out, but only a hyper-logical person would feel the need to note that) over feeling, in a way that logic or reason just cannot endure or live up to.

But engaging with and refuting her sisters causes Cordelia to follow up on the thought in an increasingly harmful way, because it leads her next to claim that love is a finite good one divides up into ever-diminishing portions: "Haply, when I shall wed,/That lord whose hand must take my plight shall carry/Half my love with him, half my care and duty" (*King Lear* 1.1.110-113). In the context of her betrothal, and in the midst of being told to tell her father she loves him, she instead claims that she is about to love him half as much as she has up until that point. Never mind the awful timing and tactics here, it is again simply not true, based on any theory or experience we have of love. If it were, families with large numbers of children would love them less than do parents of only children, and the love would steadily decrease with each new birth. (Of course, this is exactly how a firstborn child experiences the trauma of a new sibling being added and therefore subtracting from the amount of attention he or she receives from the parents, but it needn't be the reality behind that subjective experience.) Love seems much better described as expanding to include more persons (where the kind of love is the same, as in adding more children to a family), or as having different kinds of love possible from one person toward others in different roles and relationships. Again, the description of love here is perfectly reasonable, but is not therefore accurate.

Cordelia, who clearly knows what love is, based on how she behaves (i.e., lovingly) toward her father for the rest of the play, tries ineffectually to reason about it. Meanwhile, Goneril and Regan try more effectively to use reason to justify hateful, harmful behavior toward their father, and Lear tries ineffectively to counter them with some mixture of reason and sarcasm, while the Fool is content just to mock them:

GONERIL
Not only, sir, this your all-licensed Fool,
But other of your insolent retinue
Do hourly carp and quarrel, breaking forth
In rank and not-to-be-endurèd riots. Sir,
I had thought by making this well known unto you
To have found a safe redress, but now grow fearful,
By what yourself too late have spoke and done,

That you protect this course and put it on
By your allowance; which if you should, the fault
Would not 'scape censure, nor the redresses sleep
Which in the tender of a wholesome weal
Might in their working do you that offense,
Which else were shame, that then necessity
Will call discreet proceeding.

FOOL
For you know, nuncle,
The hedge-sparrow fed the cuckoo so long,
That it's had it head bit off by it young.
So out went the candle, and we were left darkling.

LEAR
Are you our daughter?

GONERIL
I would you would make use of your good wisdom,
Whereof I know you are fraught, and put away
These dispositions which of late transport you
From what you rightly are.

FOOL
May not an ass know when the cart draws the
horse? Whoop, Jug, I love thee!

LEAR
Does any here know me? This is not Lear.
Does Lear walk thus, speak thus? Where are his eyes?
Either his notion weakens, his discernings
Are lethargied—Ha! Waking? 'Tis not so.
Who is it that can tell me who I am?

FOOL
Lear's shadow.

LEAR
I would learn that, for, by the marks of sovereignty,
Knowledge, and reason, I should be false persuaded
I had daughters.

FOOL
Which they will make an obedient father.

LEAR
Your name, fair gentlewoman?

(*KL* 1.4.206-243)

Lear, the Fool, and Goneril all know exactly what is going on in this exchange, even while their styles of speech are so vastly different from one another. Goneril claims to be following "discreet proceeding," of how a household is to be run, that it should be "wholesome" and not prone to "riots." She is a Karen (in modern slang), running the Homeowners Association and patrolling the neighborhood, to keep people from having lawn signs or potted plants outside, or playing bagpipe music too loudly, while the properly upbeat and appropriately tasteful sign in her living room proclaims, "Live. Laugh. Love." The Fool rightly unpacks her claim: the sparrow's nest ceases to have "riots" in it, it becomes calm and quiet, when the cuckoo grows big enough to murder and eat its adoptive parent. And first Lear but then Goneril also quickly picks up on the real implications of that parable that this exchange is about Lear's (and Goneril's) identity: "From what you rightly are .... Who is it that can tell me who I am?" Because if Lear is treated just according to reason, then it is exactly as Goneril says: it is unreasonable to let an overly emotional, stubborn old man run around unsupervised.[2] He could get hurt, after all. But that is only if he is just any old man, and she is just some unrelated "gentlewoman." If he is still her father, and she his daughter, then something more than reason—or the survival of the fittest, as shown by the cuckoo—should be in play. But it is not. (Goneril does not here call him father, or appeal to their bond to convince him she is right.) Or even the reversal of such is being imposed, as the Fool observes, that Goneril wants to turn Lear into the oxymoron of "an obedient father," and this would be to make him into something like a ghost, no longer fully alive or human, "Lear's shadow."

Along the way, Goneril explicitly appeals to "wisdom," contrasting it with the Fool's perspective, and asking her father to follow wisdom and not the Fool. She continues this appeal in her next speech and we see more of what "wisdom" here means to her:

GONERIL
This admiration, sir, is much o' th' savor
Of other your new pranks. I do beseech you
To understand my purposes aright.
As you are old and reverend, should be wise.
Here do you keep a hundred knights and squires,
Men so disordered, so debauched and bold,
That this our court, infected with their manners,
Shows like a riotous inn. Epicurism and lust
Makes it more like a tavern or a brothel
Than a graced palace. The shame itself doth speak
For instant remedy. Be then desired,
By her that else will take the thing she begs,
A little to disquantity your train,
And the remainders that shall still depend
To be such men as may besort your age,
Which know themselves and you.

LEAR
Darkness and devils!—
Saddle my horses. Call my train together.
Some exit.
Degenerate bastard, I'll not trouble thee.
Yet have I left a daughter.

(*KL* 1.4.244-264)

Goneril is pretty openly embracing the cuckoo comparison, and no longer making much pretense of asking, but now demanding and threatening ("By her that else will take the thing she begs"), as Lear's explosive reaction makes clear. Goneril acknowledges her father is "old and reverend," but questions whether he is "wise"—and if he is not, then he will be forced to do what she says. So "wise" here really means little more than submissive (because resistance would be futile and therefore foolish). She reminds him repeatedly of his age, where age does not confer respect or deference, but only weakness and dependence.[3] Whatever followers Goneril allows her father still to have must be "men as may besort your age,/Which know themselves and you." Lear is being told to show the wisdom of knowing himself, where knowing himself means accepting his powerlessness and irrelevance, and agreeing to consort only with similarly powerless old people. As in our chapter on nature, a realization of weakness (but not irrelevance or loneliness) is always traumatic and difficult, but can be revelatory and empowering, when pursued and embraced freely by the one seeking enlightenment. When forced on someone out of malice and to control, subjugate, and belittle them, then such "tough love" is just abusive and destructive, however seemingly reasonable may be the requests to avoid "riotous ... Epicurism."

Goneril continues such praise of supposed "wisdom" when her husband expresses some hesitation or misgivings about how she is treating her father:

GONERIL
... No, no, my lord,
This milky gentleness and course of yours,
Though I condemn not, yet, under pardon,
You are much more at task for want of wisdom
Than praised for harmful mildness.

(*KL* 1.4.362-367)

Compassion or restraint or even pity are all just a lack of wisdom for such as she, and can be equated with "harmful mildness." Again, "tough love" is exactly what Goneril claims here that she is not taking away her father's dignity just to assert herself and establish her own power, but is really looking out for his safety and comfort, as well as everyone else's in the castle.

All this whittling away of Lear's entourage culminates when Goneril and Regan together very reasonably tell him he will no longer have any followers, regardless of where he stays or goes:

LEAR
Is this well spoken?

REGAN
I dare avouch it, sir. What, fifty followers?
Is it not well? What should you need of more?
Yea, or so many, sith that both charge and danger
Speak 'gainst so great a number? How in one house

Should many people under two commands
Hold amity? 'Tis hard, almost impossible.

GONERIL
Why might not you, my lord, receive attendance
From those that she calls servants, or from mine?

REGAN
Why not, my lord? If then they chanced to slack you,
We could control them. If you will come to me
(For now I spy a danger), I entreat you
To bring but five-and-twenty. To no more
Will I give place or notice.

LEAR
I gave you all—

REGAN
And in good time you gave it.

LEAR
Made you my guardians, my depositaries,
But kept a reservation to be followed
With such a number. What, must I come to you
With five-and-twenty? Regan, said you so?

REGAN
And speak 't again, my lord. No more with me.

LEAR
Those wicked creatures yet do look well-favored
When others are more wicked. Not being the worst
Stands in some rank of praise. *To Goneril.* I'll go with thee.
Thy fifty yet doth double five-and-twenty,
And thou art twice her love.

GONERIL
Hear me, my lord.
What need you five-and-twenty, ten, or five,

To follow in a house where twice so many
Have a command to tend you?

REGAN
What need one?

(*KL* 2.4.271-303)

Everything Goneril and Regan say is reasonable, and is presented as such. Lear does not need followers, the way he needs food and shelter. But of course Goneril and Regan and Lear know that by reducing his allowable needs to just those of physical survival, they are reducing him to an animal existence.[4] They are not only not treating him as king (which he is no longer, and could be blamed for having given away), but they are not even treating him as their father or as an elderly man (intrinsic statuses of respect he could not relinquish, though Goneril and Regan believe they can deny all implications of them).

Interesting, too, that in this exchange at such a crucial turning point in the play, we return to something like Cordelia's idea that love is quantifiable and can be measured, split, and doled out among people ("Thy fifty yet doth double five-and-twenty,/ And thou art twice her love"). But here, in context, the idea is much more grotesque, because Lear announces this following on his hideous cursing of Goneril that we already examined. It is an explosive and heartrending scene, because our sympathies for Lear should be at their highest: he's being treated literally like a useless, dangerous, wild animal by his daughters, as both Gloucester and Cordelia later note: "If wolves had at thy gate howled that stern time,/Thou shouldst have said 'Good porter, turn the key'," "Mine enemy's dog,/Though he had bit me, should have stood that night/Against my fire" (*King Lear* 3.7.76-78; 4.7.42-44). But he is simultaneously showing his worst, most willful and stubborn obliviousness to the ugliness and venom he could also spew out on them just moments before. In the context of Goneril and Regan talking in completely reasonable but utterly grotesque terms, perhaps it is appropriate that Lear also talk in desiccated, detached, mathematical language that overlooks his own grotesque behavior. The family resemblance is remarkable and ugly.

But the play relies on simple lines as much as on its more complex speeches,[5] and Regan's "What need one?" are three of the most chilling syllables ever. The façade of reasonability is perhaps still there but it is brutal in its minimalism. The question is completely rhetorical, as long as one accepts Goneril and Regan's brand of reasonability. But if one does not, then the question contains in it all the outrage and callous, casual brutality of abusing someone who is powerless to fight back, and Lear takes it as such:

LEAR
O, reason not the need! Our basest beggars
Are in the poorest thing superfluous.
Allow not nature more than nature needs,
Man's life is cheap as beast's. Thou art a lady;
If only to go warm were gorgeous,
Why, nature needs not what thou gorgeous wear'st,
Which scarcely keeps thee warm. But, for true need—
You heavens, give me that patience, patience I need!
You see me here, you gods, a poor old man
As full of grief as age, wretched in both.
If it be you that stirs these daughters' hearts
Against their father, fool me not so much
To bear it tamely. Touch me with noble anger,
And let not women's weapons, water drops,
Stain my man's cheeks.—No, you unnatural hags,
I will have such revenges on you both
That all the world shall—I will do such things—
What they are yet I know not, but they shall be
The terrors of the Earth! You think I'll weep.
No, I'll not weep.
I have full cause of weeping, but this heart
Storm and tempest.
Shall break into a hundred thousand flaws
Or ere I'll weep.—O Fool, I shall go mad!

(*KL* 2.4.304-327)

Lear takes the implications quickly to their conclusions: to offer reasons at a time like this, between people who are supposed to love one another, is worse than to miss the point. It is to introduce other points than love and humanity, and pursue those instead. Human life, even of the lowest, economically and socially, cannot exist with just the bare subsistence level of needs: "Our basest beggars/Are in the poorest thing superfluous." To deny that and to keep a person just fed and sheltered, is to reduce them and force them to become an animal: "Allow not nature more than nature needs,/Man's life is cheap as beast's."[6] (And living in an America where we cage children and allow them just the barest necessities of survival, while congratulating ourselves on our greatness and exceptionalism, I feel this line more keenly than I have before.) Again, we are back to the issues around clothing, which animals do not wear, and humans do not *need* to wear (in the sense of physical survival), but they do so in order to show they are human (and show what kind of human they are). As long as the conversation is about reasons and needs, it is not about *human* life, really. Lear mostly realizes that here (so long as it is a matter of someone using reason to mistreat him), but he himself has to get further from reason in the storm scenes, as we have seen.[7]

The rest of this speech by Lear turns to the issue of his weeping, a very different form of expression than reasoned discourse and debate. But if Lear has rejected his daughters' reasoned and evil way of treating him, then the irrational or non-rational kind of expression that weeping is, may be the right kind of expression in this situation. Lear is right finally, to weep at what has been done to him, but even more right to weep for what he did. That he (like Augustine) is unable to weep when needed and appropriate is a telling symptom of their lack of mental and spiritual health at those points in their lives. It is the false fetishization of reason and denigration of "mere" emotion that sickens both men (and in the case of Lear, his daughters are far worse, so here we do not have some gender essentialism, but rather some falsifying idea of power and control over oneself and others that men may be more prone to, but is in no way unique to them).

"O reason not the need!" in some ways summarizes both our texts on the problem of reason. One cannot reason about needs (though one can and should reason how and whether to obtain what one needs). They are too basic and given.[8] And even as the basic categories of needs are universal, their particular expressions are individual and subjective. So, for example here, even Goneril and Regan would probably claim that their father is "reverend" and deserves respect, but they are reasoning how to show that respect, and what they end up claiming as reasonable is anything but virtuous or respectful. And for Lear and Cordelia, to reason about love is to end up with some grotesque explanation of it that is unrecognizable—either as some finite quantity one doles out, as Cordelia tries wrongly to explain it in the opening scene, or as something that is demanded and spoken of, clearly and unambiguously, as Lear attempts to extort it. Love in the play is the highest need, and does not admit of such explanations or manipulations.

Of course it is this for Augustine, too, but just taken to the theist's highest yearning—the love of God, the love that exceeds all others, but also makes all other loves possible, the love to which all others contribute, ultimately, if they are done rightly, and from which they detract, if they are sinful. I think in his narrative of his life and how he believes he came to love God as rightly as he could, Augustine shows that, as in *King Lear*, reason is just not sufficient for the most important and uniquely human needs. There was never any doctrine or debate or proof that could be shown to him, that would convince him to love and trust God. But once one introduces the idea of a Being such as God, then reason will have to play a bigger role than it does in the world envisioned in *King Lear* (where gods or God are possible but by no means certain). Reason's role, however, is to exhaust itself and admit it not only does not know some things, it simply cannot know some (and some of the most important, at that). Somewhat analogously to how Lear has to find out how weak and insufficient he is, because he is human, and he can then relearn (if, optimistically, he ever knew how in the first place) how to love and rely on other weak people, internally reason has to find out its own insufficiency and rely on other faculties to know and do those things reason cannot. And most important and difficult among these, for Augustine, would be to decide to love God above all else.

Notes

1 Cf. Vaught, *Journey toward God in Augustine's* Confessions. *Books I–VI*, 123: "Second, he mentions God, who has already begun to teach him in ways that surpass his understanding (5.6.10). The second reference is more important than the first because it points to the

source of redemption that will not only lead him beyond Manichaeism, but also beyond skepticism and Neoplatonism as doctrines that transform his intellect without redeeming his will."

2 Thus McFarland, "Image of the Family," 96–7: "Unlovable though she is, Goneril here speaks in tones with which many with numerous and long-staying guests can sympathize, and we do remember that previously she has taken care to ascertain at least one of the facts .... Moreover, in the early part of the play's action she speaks in tones that at least attempt to justify her conduct."

3 Cf. Morris, *Shakespeare's God*, 360: "The ingrained habits of rule appear to them as dispositions that transport him from what he rightly is; in the eyes of authority, the wisdom of one so old and reverend must be to conform to the wills of those holding power. They ask of Lear simply that, being weak, he should seem so."

4 Cf. Basney, "Is a Christian Perspective on Shakespeare Productive and/or Necessary?" 32: "In 2.4 the sisters are scrupulously, icily polite, even solicitous, as they ignore what is staring them in the face, that they are stripping Lear of his self."

5 Cf. Edelstein, *Thinking Shakespeare*, 131: "One of the most wonderful things to discover about Shakespeare as you work on his plays is that the vast majority of his language is not poetical at all. An enormous amount of it—one could even say the majority—is simple, straightforward, and unadorned."

6 Cf. Boitani, *Gospel according to Shakespeare*, 27, who connects this speech to Job: "There is little doubt that from his words emerges the so-called Joban paradigm, the self-identification of the king with his biblical predecessor, victim of God."

7 Cf. Boitani, *Gospel according to Shakespeare*, 30: "To understand how things truly are, Lear is forced to lose his reason totally."

8 Cf. Williams, *Tragic Imagination*, 39: "If we are going to speak of debts—she [Cordelia] implies—then the level of 'payment' is simply a *given*. Price and value are not to be haggled over, and there is no possible ground for a bidding war in love" (emphasis in original).

Conclusion: The Problem of Resolution

We have examined four major problems of being human, on which these two texts help shed light. There are surely others, and other pairs of texts we could have used. But for these, I feel, a surprising and uplifting level of unity has emerged, between the two texts, and connecting the different problems, seeing how they related to one another, how patterns and connections recurred throughout our discussion. In a way, everything kept revolving back to love. Given how both texts begin—a father demanding his daughters say they love him, a middle-aged man thinking back on a career and loves and deaths that have led him to think his heart can only find its true love in God—this enormous, inescapable gravity of love in these stories is anything but surprising. But I don't think we would have gotten quite the consistency or harmony from other duets on love, though I am amusing myself here at the end, thinking of how disparate and exciting some pairs could be—Baudelaire and Dante, Sappho and Flannery O'Connor. But with the odd couple we have spent our time with, there was way more mutuality and support than I had expected. There were interruptions or complications to communicating love (the problem of language) or thinking about it (the problem of reason). And our longest chapter by far (the problem of nature) showed that we kept coming back to love because both texts conceived of it as built-in to humans (whether by God or not may make some difference in part of our discussion now, but not on this point, of its being innate), but built-in, in such a way that it caused enormous problems, pain, and suffering. Love stinks, or love hurts, or love is a battlefield—I could give popular song lyrics all day that would tend to support this part of the observation. But they would also all agree that love is that in which we find the highest fulfillment and happiness in our lives.

As illuminating as all that would be, however, one more question nags: if so conflicted, by nature, about love, the ultimate or even only source of our joy, is there any possibility of lasting happiness for humans, according to these texts? The surviving main characters of *King Lear* seem to think not:

KENT
Is this the promised end?

EDGAR
Or image of that horror?

ALBANY
Fall and cease.

(*KL* 5.3.316-318)

Bloom, who for all his cranky arrogance and snarky condescension, has been an excellent companion for me on this journey (a mentor, really, though we never met), is even more explicit: "Love redeems nothing—on this Shakespeare could not be clearer—but the powerful representation of love askew, thwarted, misunderstood, or turned into hatred or icy indifference (Goneril, Regan, Edmund) can become an uncanny aesthetic value."[1] But if I can confess that the so-called conversion scene of *Confessions* has always left me cold,[2] I can now say the same of "aesthetic value." I don't know what that would be, on its own, devoid of other kinds of meaning (moral, psychological, spiritual, intellectual, etc.), or why I would long for or pursue it, if overwhelming sadness was all I left the theater with. I would then have to agree with Augustine, that theater going (or drama reading) was "incredible stupidity" (*Conf.* 3.2.2), and I don't think I do, really.[3]

Of course, it could be simply that here is one point, finally, on which the pesky matter of belief in God does make a difference, as much as I have tried to gloss that—not out of misrepresentation, I hope, so much as from a deeply held belief of my own, that such belief ultimately doesn't make as much difference as both believers and non-believers love to rail and scold about. I have been both (believer and non-) in my life, and noticed almost no difference in quality of life or how I lived or what I valued. Or whom I loved, since we're on that subject. (Though there were times, in retrospect, when I think it made a large and painful difference in how or whether someone loved me.) So I'm not as committed to Augustine and Shakespeare parting ways on this last topic, as some might be. But I also will try hard not to force them into agreement here, if it's not warranted.

Perhaps not surprisingly, I will say I think they mostly agree, even on this issue of human happiness, with one slight but crucial difference—and yes, that small but important difference is because God looms so large in the one text, and is left as an abiding question mark, in the other. There are two scenes, late in both narratives, in which the male protagonist is finally alone, calm, at peace, in the midst of a hostile world, with a woman he loves, and who (more importantly, I'd say) loves him unconditionally, who has gone to some enormous and costly lengths to do so, to stand by him when he was at his more insufferable, arrogant, demanding, and hostile. With Lear, he is briefly happy and reunited with Cordelia:

LEAR
No, no, no, no. Come, let's away to prison.
We two alone will sing like birds i' th' cage.
When thou dost ask me blessing, I'll kneel down
And ask of thee forgiveness. So we'll live,
And pray, and sing, and tell old tales, and laugh
At gilded butterflies, and hear poor rogues
Talk of court news, and we'll talk with them too—
Who loses and who wins; who's in, who's out—
And take upon 's the mystery of things,
As if we were God's spies. And we'll wear out,
In a walled prison, packs and sects of great ones
That ebb and flow by th' moon.

EDMUND
Take them away.

LEAR
Upon such sacrifices, my Cordelia,

The gods themselves throw incense. Have I caught thee?
He that parts us shall bring a brand from heaven
And fire us hence like foxes. Wipe thine eyes.
The good years shall devour them, flesh and fell,
Ere they shall make us weep. We'll see 'em starved first.
Come.

(*KL* 5.3.9-30)

As I've noted with Lear, his lines always ring true, because there's always plenty of the "old" Lear (misguided, self-centered, oblivious), even as he rhapsodizes in a new mode (of compassion, selflessness, self-awareness). Consistent, he ain't (except to be consistently inconsistent), but I take that as no indictment of Shakespeare's art, but rather a profound confirmation of skill and insight beyond most any other author, because that is how real people talk—with continuity, as they change, with new insights, even as they stay partially anchored to aspects and bits of their past. So here Lear seems oddly trapped in an imagined good version of the opening scene ("When thou dost ask me blessing, I'll kneel down/And ask of thee forgiveness"). I'm not sure that's the healthiest, most wholesome version of love that I'd want to imagine for myself—an endless, *Groundhog Day* like repetition of a scene that went terribly wrong in real life because of my bad actions, but if it could only play out correctly, I'd want it repeated over and over ad infinitum. But from there I do see some progress for Lear. "And pray, and sing, and tell old tales, and laugh," sounds more like a natural, joyful life with a beloved. There's also the implied rejection of Lear's former life in court that we saw before in our analysis: "and hear poor rogues/Talk of court news." Such a false life Lear and Cordelia will observe from a safe distance, caged off from it and its constantly changing pain and mortality: "And we'll wear out,/In a walled prison packs and sects of great ones/That ebb and flow by th' moon." And there is finally some inkling or glimpse of God—but more importantly, of being with God, of being in God's employ and under God's direction and guidance, and not just basking in the presence of the human beloved: "And take upon 's the mystery of things,/As if we were God's spies."

But that "As if" hangs over the whole scene: this is all a hope, or even just a fantasy. If there is happiness in *King Lear*, it is in the beautiful moments spent with a real, sincerely, selflessly loved person, but such moments are as fleeting as any flower or butterfly any other poet has contemplated and praised.[4] Hell, more so—those beautiful objects of nature last days; the idyll with Lear and Cordelia seems measured more in minutes or, at most, hours. These moments yearn for or give intimations of something eternal, as we saw all the way back when we examined how France spoke of the gods when he first felt love for Cordelia. So, "Love redeems nothing,"[5] seems a bit too categorical and final to me.[6] Love shows what redemption would be, were such a thing possible for the beautiful, awful creatures we are. And for most of us, those moments, and the possibilities—in ourselves, in others, in the universe—of which they make us aware, are worth all the pain of getting to them.[7]

But temporary and fleeting they are, in a world such as the play envisions, and to which it relentlessly, mercilessly brings us back, every hopeful step or speech notwithstanding.[8] In that respect, Augustine's equivalent scene, the rapturous vision of God he shares with his mother Monica, is both similar and different:

> Our colloquy led us to the point where the pleasures of the body's senses, however intense and in however brilliant a material light enjoyed, seemed unworthy not merely of comparison but even of remembrance beside the joy of that life, and we lifted ourselves in longing yet more ardent toward *That Which Is*, and step by step traversed all bodily creatures and heaven itself, whence sun and moon and stars shed their light upon the earth. Higher still we mounted by inward thought and wondering discourse on your works, and we arrived at the summit of our own minds; and this too we transcended, to touch that land of never-failing plenty where you pasture Israel for ever with the food of truth. Life there is the Wisdom through whom all these things are made, and all others that have been or ever will be; but Wisdom herself is not made: she is as she always has been and will be for ever. Rather should we say that in her there is no "has been" or "will be," but only being, for she is eternal, but past and future do not belong to eternity. And as we talked and panted for it, we just touched the edge of it by the utmost leap of our hearts; then, sighing and unsatisfied, we left the first-fruits of our spirit captive there, and returned to the noises of articulate speech, where a word has a beginning and end. How different from your Word, our Lord, who abides in himself, and grows not old, but renews all things. (*Conf.* 9.10.24)

Perfectly analogous is the description of the descent back into the "regular" world, as a fall back into a world full of "the noises of articulate speech." How telling, to label human speech as nothing but noise. That is exactly the world Cordelia eschewed (whether out of idealism or pride or both), exactly the world Goneril and Regan and Edmund thrived in, and exactly the one Augustine and Lear learned (gently for the former, violently and painfully for the latter) to flee and condemn.

But Augustine's vision of moments with the beloved is different than Lear's fantasy of life with his beloved. Augustine and Monica quickly fly past "the pleasures of the body's senses," into some realm of pure "thought and wondering discourse." And while Lear does not imagine eating bon-bons with Cordelia (to take a gross example of "the pleasures of the body's senses"), he does imagine a world in which the particularities of Cordelia and himself are still maintained: he blesses, she forgives, they both laugh and sing and listen to the kinds of people who had previously plagued their existence. I think it is absolutely crucial to Augustine's vision of blessedness that he is there with someone he loves (and someone he repeatedly, habitually belittled and wronged), but the specifics of her or of their relationship are not part of the vision or the happiness (just part of why they're there together, experiencing that joy).[9] To be very clear: earthly joys and loves lead one to a transcendent, heavenly joy and love. Augustine is not about rejecting or denying such earthly, human loves; but when the visionary's willful blinders come off, and the earthly loves and beauties point beyond themselves (as they must, if they are holy and not hellish) the gaze and happiness fall on something not earthly, but on "*That Which Is*" and then, "Wisdom herself."[10] Lear is momentarily happy, because he and Cordelia can briefly love each other without fault or mistake. Augustine is happy, because he and his mother loved and even saw God together, and that temporary ecstasy was based on—and for Augustine, reliably and faithfully leads to—eternal union with that God.

That then changes not just the content of the vision, but also its outcome or aftermath, and the permanence and eternity of the happiness it offers. Lear cannot hold on to a happiness with an earthly, mortal beloved, not just because Edmund is there, hurrying them along to their planned deaths, but because of the nature of what he loves: a mortal, finite being engenders and enflames a finite, temporary love and happiness. But although Augustine slips back into the world of mere "noise," he does so fully convinced that that world is the impermanent, fleeting, and false one. The eternal and true world, of which properly ordered and embraced human loves give a momentary taste, "first-fruits," is the real world, and it is created, filled, and renewed by the Word of God, which is God and our Lord.

So how close are these two texts on human happiness? They both conceive of it as only possible by loving others, and doing so while owning one's own unworthiness. For *King Lear*, such happiness is fleeting at best, though it gives glimpses of eternal realities and bliss that are possible but never finally confirmed (or denied) in the play.[11] For Augustine, the fleeting happiness of seeing God with one's beloved (who is beloved because she, too, loves God), is a brief experience of what eternal happiness will be like, and it is only achieved through total faith that it will be eternal. To me they seem indistinguishable—and indistinguishably beautiful, really—in how they praise human loves. If I had to guess, finally, why I was drawn back to these two texts and not others, that would be why: I have never felt my own joys and frustrations with human love so reflected back to me in a text, as I have with these two. In the final outcome or ultimate source of such love they are hugely different. But perhaps I am finally more practical than I'd like to admit: if two texts agree on what love is and how it feels and what it spurs us to do (good and bad), then its source and final end (which are, to be honest, totally unknowable by us humans), are of merely academic interest, and hardly worth quibbling over, when such deep currents of agreement are there to be examined and enjoyed.

As I began this book with personal reflections on how I came to write it, let me end with some on what that writing has now revealed to me. As I noted at the beginning, these two texts have been with me frequently throughout the last thirty-five years—most of my life, all of my adult life. That helped account for why I would write about them now, why I might think I have something to say about them. No matter how dull my mind might be, thirty-five years of practice and engagement with these texts and with students talking and writing about them should have yielded some interesting observations. Hopefully that has been borne out in these pages.

But as I have been writing this, and thinking deeply about these texts—or just as often, thinking about how I've thought about these texts, and how others thought, and how I thought about their thinking—it came into much clearer focus, how differently I've related to them over these many years, thus returning to some of the problems of time that I tried to unpack in my Introduction. It is not just in the obvious (I hope) observation that I'm more careful and mature now in how I analyze them. I'm not smarter than I was in 1986 but I know a lot more, and bring that added knowledge, as well as many more experiences, to my reading and reflection. It is the myriad experiences that I have stumbled into over the past thirty-five years that most fascinate me now at the end of this process and convince me that pairing these two texts makes perfect sense to me today, in ways it would not have at any point before. It dawned on me first in poring over Lear's speeches. In more recent rereadings of the play, I had felt more connection to him than I had as a younger reader, and I remember distinctly last fall, "I gave you all" (*King Lear* 2.4.286), which needn't be a particularly emotional line, unexpectedly had me choking up (in class no less, I'm sure to the amusement and/or alarm of 25 eighteen-year-olds).[12] It had only been during the last couple years, I realized, that I identified most with Lear in the play, and I think it almost comes down to that line, so much simpler and less adorned than his more famous speeches. Once one goes all in with identifying with Lear, much of the play comes down to feeling his pain at giving things away (of course the territories on the map at the beginning, but more mysteriously and lingeringly, all the odd stuff about clothes throughout, never mind all the bodies strewn about him at the end), and learning, painfully, to give some things away in such a way that is finally uplifting and not degrading, fulfilling and not annihilating—of becoming "unburdened" (*King Lear* 1.1.43) in a way that is enlivening, not fatal (if such is even possible, and the play is evocative but not definitive on this). "Well, dear, life is a casting off," Linda calmly or even cheerfully tells Willy very near the beginning of *Death of a Salesman* (a more recent addition to what I teach freshmen),[13] but of course he clings to his old life (or his falsified memories of it, really), even more stubbornly than Lear. I was nearly weeping in class that afternoon because I very much felt for and with Lear, that all the giving or casting off he and I had been doing in adulthood, hadn't amounted to much, really. (And yes, I'm aware of how much this all hearkens back to my description of my own father in my Introduction, and how he let things go perhaps too easily, and seemed to have finally an almost unnatural kind of lonely independence, free of all attachments.) I'm sure there are many kinds of regrets in middle or old age, and I don't think mine line up perfectly with Lear's, but I've felt a special sympathy for him recently.

And as I reflected back on many earlier readings of the play, I not only realized how differently I had read it before, but how it is so carefully built to draw us in, in quite different ways, all of them so variously powerful and engaging. I realized now, which I hadn't known at the time, how much more I had identified with Cordelia when younger. I think I had always seen some of my father in Lear—needy, demanding, fragile, incapable of expressing emotions other than anger—and may have known, inchoately and instinctively, that such identification accounted for some of my abiding fascination with the play.[14] But it was only recently that, looking back, I could see that unlike other admirable female characters whose stories I have taught many times (e.g., Antigone and Beatrice immediately come to mind, as does Monica, especially in the current context), I did not just admire Cordelia (as I do those others),[15] but I identified so deeply and intimately with her plight of feeling too much and saying too little, being unable to make ourselves understood, when surrounded by people who are either glib or domineering or both. There are many texts and characters I love as much as *King Lear* and its eponymous father and his youngest daughter, but it's much harder to think of ones that have so fit into my own life, that I would identify with one major character when younger, and gradually transition in middle age to seeing myself in another. The often observed opposite case of this, for many of us, is how *Catcher in the Rye* fails to make this transition. Many of us identify so powerfully with Holden when we are sixteen, but the intensity of the identification is in inverse proportion to its longevity, and when we return later to the book (if we refuse to heed others' warnings not to), it is a painful embarrassment. With really great literature, and characters of greater complexity, this is perhaps felt less extremely, but I think it is a pattern I've seen repeated many times, but which this play has uncannily (and quite unnoticed by me until now) managed to evade, staying with me more closely than other literature as I aged, and now reminding me of my younger self and my parentage, even as it counsels and sympathizes with me in my current situation. As I say, uncanny is the best word for it, and certainly not something I ever realized before now.

But since I've been working so closely with both *King Lear* and *Confessions*, this observation made me see now that something similar had happened with *Confessions*. Not that I had identified with different characters in it, over many readings (Augustine is pretty myopically focused on himself throughout: the supporting cast does not get enough detail for us to identify with them, really), but that the extended time period of the narrative (*c*. 33 years) had given me many possible Augustines, each typified by some critical scene, to focus on over the years.[16] I confess I have not yet experienced the frame of mind that would draw me into the scene in the garden of Book Eight, which makes me perhaps a very odd spokesperson or fan of the book, as I have yet to ever quite "get" the crucial, climactic scene. Or perhaps it makes me a better one, as the deep impressions made on me by many, various scenes are more equal and memorable and fascinating to me. Augustine's vivid, detailed descriptions of how he reacted to the deaths of his friend and his mother held me enthralled when I was younger, so painfully close were they to similar experiences of my own, from so many years ago (though quite close to when I first read the book). And now? Now I see so much more clearly (though I still can't hold on to it with the firmness and confidence that Augustine claims to), why and how he'd feel compelled to write such a book. Looking back on a life and gathering together what now seem the important parts, the sad and joyful and confusing parts, and stringing them into some kind of order that one claims makes sense, and confessing all of them to God as paradoxical, undeserved blessings—well, I think that is what I'm doing in my better, happier moments, when I'm not raging or weeping like Lear over all that has slipped or been given away. Writing this book has been a good bit of both, the raging and the confessing, and I thank you for joining me on the journey. I hope it was a profitable detour on yours.

Notes

1 Bloom, *Shakespeare*, 506.
2 I am encouraged that others see its importance overstated by readers/interpreters of *Confessions*. See Miles, *Augustine and the*

Fundamentalist's Daughter, 144–5: "In fact, the *Confessions* is all about the gradual and cumulative shift in his intellectual, emotional, and erotic attractions." See also Wills, *Saint Augustine's Conversion*, 5: "Of course, conversion in the broad sense does not necessarily entail a change of creed. It can refer to any significant spiritual reorientation (whether sudden or gradual). In that sense, Augustine's life up to the garden scene was one long tale of conversions."

3 Cf. Williams, *Tragic Imagination*, 43–4: "If one aspect of tragic representation is simply the affirmation that something can be spoken rather than locked in total silence, beyond words and meaning, another is that experiencing extreme pain does not automatically make one deaf to the atrocity another is experiencing."

4 Cf. Clifford Davidson, "History of *King Lear* and the Problem of Belief," *Christianity and Literature* 45 (1996): 285–301, esp. 296, that Shakespeare's "point is the remarkably Christian conclusion that in this world there is no continuing city and that we are 'strangers and sojourners' (see Lev. 25:23) without expectation of the cessation of intrigue or war- fare in the here and now."

5 Bloom, *Shakespeare*, 506.

6 And cf. such analyses as Hackett, "'And Thou, all-shaking Thunder'," "Hence: this is only the beginning of the play, a setting of the stage for a descent and return from madness; though a tragedy, it is also a tale of salvation." Also McFarland, "Image of the Family," 108: "And yet not even in these outpourings of joy and wonder is the emotion as powerful as in the awesome reconciliation scene between Lear and Cordelia. Lear's awakening from madness into rationality is, on the literal plane, a moment of restoration, reconciliation, and reunion. But on the anagogical plane it is more; it is the reawakening of the dead into paradise."

7 Cf. Mack, "The World of *King Lear*," 69: "And what we are and may be was never, I submit, more memorably fixed upon the stage than in this kneeling old man whose heartbreak is precisely the measure of what, in our world of relatedness, it is possible to lose and possible to win .... When we come crying hither, we bring with us the badge of all our misery; but it is also the badge of the vulnerabilities that give us access to whatever grandeur we achieve." See also McFarland, "Image of the Family," 107: "But possibly the most unmistakable index of the centrality of family kinesis in Shakespeare's concern is the scene in the fourth act of *King Lear* where Lear is reunited with Cordelia. Such a theme of reunion, especially of the reunion of a family—or, as here, the living heart of a family—mines the deepest and richest lode of Shakespeare's affirmation of life; and that truth is apparent in other places than

King Lear." Also Mark Schwehn, "*King Lear* beyond Reason," *First Things* 36 (1993): 25–33; online at https://www.firstthings.com/article/1993/10/king-lear-beyond-reason-love-and-justice-in-the-family: "On this side of eternity, there are at best fleeting though magnificent moments of glad grace, such as the one we witness between Lear and Cordelia. Although such moments are vastly more redemptive than anything else in the world of *Lear*, they are finally unworldly, in the world but not of it."

8 Cf. Williams, *Tragic Imagination*, 40: "Shakespeare is clearly not interested in a consoling ending of any sort, but equally it is not obvious that the ending is in itself a refutation of what has happened before .... The questions left are whether the play's underlying diagnosis of (some of) the roots of suffering in denial and fiction is true, and whether the reconciliation of Lear and Cordelia, and Lear's partial regeneration, are any less significant for being transient."

9 Cf. the very apposite summation of Wills, *Saint Augustine's Conversion*, 9: "On the basis of his new respect for Monnica, the mystical experience he shared with this unlettered woman ... is meant to destroy the presumption that soul-culture demands exercise in the liberal arts .... Monnica did not lead him to baptism. Rather, baptism led him to Monnica."

10 Cf. Miles, *Augustine and the Fundamentalist's Daughter*, 125: "I found that Plotinus and Augustine shared the problem of the ambiguity of bodies, *both* 'lowest rung' on the ladder of value and *starting place* for spiritual ascent. Both professed respect and admiration for bodies, but both could, on occasion, also insist that bodies are distracting and must be 'overlooked', literally, looked over" (emphasis in original).

11 Cf. Boitani, *Gospel according to Shakespeare*, 5, 26: "No such consummation is allowed either to Hamlet or to Lear and Cordelia .... it is only for a brief moment that Lear is offered restoration."

12 Cf. Bloom, *Shakespeare*, 513: "To feel what Lear suffers strains us as only our own greatest anguishes have hurt us; the terrible intimacy that Lear insists upon is virtually unbearable, as Dr. Johnson testified."

13 Arthur Miller, *Death of a Salesman* (New York: Penguin Books, 1976; first published 1949), 15.

14 Cf. Bloom, *Shakespeare*, 513: "I have argued already that this intimacy stems from Lear's usurpation of everyone's experience of ambivalence toward the father, or toward fatherhood .... Lear the father, thanks to Shakespeare's audacity, endlessly evokes God the Father, a Western metaphor now repudiated in all of our academies and in our more enlightened churches."

15 Cf. Boitani, *Gospel according to Shakespeare*, 8: "An integral part of such an overall design is the role played by women. The Gospel according to Shakespeare is wonderfully inflected and proclaimed in feminine form."

16 Cf. Miles, *Augustine and the Fundamentalist's Daughter*, 23: "Somebody wise has said that each of us is our own favorite character in fiction. We tell ourselves, in constant interior self-talk, a story about who we are that helps us get by, or flourish, or that limits or even destroys us as we set out to prove that the story we tell ourselves is an accurate story."

BIBLIOGRAPHY

Adelman, Janet. "Introduction." In *Twentieth Century Interpretations of King Lear: A Collection of Critical Essays*. Edited by Janet Adelman. Englewood Cliffs, NJ: Prentice-Hall, 1978. Pp. 1–21.

Augustine. *The Confessions*. The Works of Saint Augustine: A Translation for the 21st Century. Translated by Maria Boulding. Hyde Park, NY: New City Press, 2001.

Barber, C. L. "On Christianity and the Family: Tragedy of the Sacred." In *Twentieth Century Interpretations of King Lear: A Collection of Critical Essays*. Edited by Janet Adelman. Englewood Cliffs, NJ: Prentice-Hall, 1978. Pp. 117–19.

Barthes, Roland. "The World of Wrestling." In *Mythologies*. New York: Hill and Wang, 1972. Pp. 15–25.

Basney, Lionel, "Is a Christian Perspective on Shakespeare Productive and/or Necessary?" In *Shakespeare and the Christian Tradition*. Edited by E. B. Batson. Lewiston, NY: Edwin Mellen Press, 1994. Pp. 19–35.

Batson, E. Beatrice, ed. *Shakespeare and the Christian Tradition*. Edited by E. B. Batson. Lewiston, NY: Edwin Mellen Press, 1994.

Bloom, Harold. *Shakespeare: The Invention of the Human*. New York: Riverhead Books, 1998.

Boitani, Piero. *The Gospel according to Shakespeare*. Translated by Vittorio Montemaggi and Rachel Jacoff. Notre Dame, IN: University of Notre Dame Press, 2013.

Booth, Stephen. "On the Greatness of *King Lear*." In *Twentieth Century Interpretations of King Lear: A Collection of Critical Essays*. Edited by Janet Adelman. Englewood Cliffs, NJ: Prentice-Hall, 1978. Pp. 98–111.

Booth, Stephen. "On the Greatness of *King Lear*." In *William Shakespeare's King Lear*. Edited by Harold Bloom. New York: Chelsea House, 1987. Pp. 57–70.

Brown, Peter. *Augustine of Hippo: A Biography*. Forty-Fifth Anniversary Edition. Berkeley and Los Angeles: University of California Press, 2000. First published, 1967.

Calderwood, James L. "Creative Uncreation in *King Lear*." In *William Shakespeare's King Lear*. Edited by Harold Bloom. New York: Chelsea House, 1987. Pp. 121–37.

Chadwick, Henry. *Augustine*. Past Masters. Oxford, New York et al.: Oxford University Press, 1986.

Danby, J. F. *Shakespeare's Doctrine of Nature: A Study of King Lear*. London: Faber & Faber, 1949.

Danson, L., ed. *On King Lear*. Princeton, NJ: Princeton University Press, 1981.

Davidson, Clifford. "History of *King Lear* and the Problem of Belief." *Christianity and Literature* 45 (1996) 285–301.

Delasanta, Rodney. "Putting off the Old Man and Putting on the New: Ephesians 4: 22-24 in Chaucer, Shakespeare, Swift, and Dostoevsky." *Christianity and Literature* 51 (2002) 339–62.

Dobell, Brian. *Augustine's Intellectual Conversion: The Journey from Platonism to Christianity*. Cambridge, UK et al.: Cambridge University Press, 2009.

Edelstein, Barry. *Thinking Shakespeare: A Working Guide for Actors, Directors, Students... and Anyone Else Interested in the Bard*. Rev. ed. New York: Theatre Communications Group, 2018.

Elton, W. R. *King Lear and the Gods*. San Marino, CA: Huntington Library, 1968.

Farrell, James M. "The Rhetoric(s) of St. Augustine's Confessions." *Augustinian Studies* 39 (2) (2008) 265–91.

Goddard, Harold C. *"King Lear."* In *William Shakespeare's King Lear*. Edited by Harold Bloom. New York: Chelsea House, 1987. Pp. 9–43.

Goldberg, S. L. "On Edgar's Character." In *Twentieth Century Interpretations of King Lear: A Collection of Critical Essays*. Edited by Janet Adelman. Englewood Cliffs, NJ: Prentice-Hall, 1978. Pp. 114–16.

Greenfield, Thelma Nelson. "The Clothing Motif in King Lear." *Shakespeare Quarterly* 5 (1954) 281–6.

Hackett, William C. "'And Thou, all-Shaking Thunder...' A Theological Notation to Lines 1–38 of *King Lear*, Act III, Scene II." *Religions* 8 (5) 2017 91. Online at https://doi.org/10.3390/rel8050091.

Harbage, Alfred, ed. *King Lear*. The Pelican Shakespeare. New York: Penguin Books, 1958 (rev. ed. 1970).

Knights, L. C. "On the Fool." In *Twentieth Century Interpretations of King Lear: A Collection of Critical Essays*. Edited by Janet Adelman. Englewood Cliffs, NJ: Prentice-Hall, 1978. Pp. 122–3.

Kolbet, Paul R. *Augustine and the Cure of Souls*. Notre Dame, IN: University of Notre Dame Press, 2010.

Kronenfeld, Judy. *King Lear and the Naked Truth: Rethinking the Language of Religion and Resistance*. Durham, NC, and London: Duke University Press, 1998.

Mack, Maynard. "The World of *King Lear*." In *Twentieth Century Interpretations of King Lear: A Collection of Critical Essays*. Edited by Janet Adelman. Englewood Cliffs, NJ: Prentice-Hall, 1978. Pp. 56–69.

Marx, S. *Shakespeare and the Bible*. New York: Oxford University Press, 2000.

McFarland, Thomas. "The Image of the Family in *King Lear*." In *On King Lear*. Edited by Lawrence Danson. Princeton, NJ: Princeton University Press, 1981. Pp. 91–118.

Miles, Margaret R. *Augustine and the Fundamentalist's Daughter*. Eugene, OR: Cascade Books, 2011.

Miller, Arthur. *Death of a Salesman*. New York: Penguin Books, 1976. First published 1949.

Morris, Ivor. *Shakespeare's God*. London: Allen and Unwin, 1971.

Muir, Kenneth. "On Christian Values." In *Twentieth Century Interpretations of King Lear: A Collection of Critical Essays*. Edited by Janet Adelman. Englewood Cliffs, NJ: Prentice-Hall, 1978. P. 120.

John L., Murphy. *Darkness and Devils: Exorcism and King Lear*. Athens, OH, and London: Ohio University Press, 1984.

Nevo, Ruth. "On Lear and Job." In *Twentieth Century Interpretations of King Lear: A Collection of Critical Essays*. Edited by Janet Adelman. Englewood Cliffs, NJ: Prentice-Hall, 1978. Pp. 120–2.

O'Donnell, James J. *Augustine: A New Biography*. New York: HarperCollins, 2005.

Paffenroth, Kim, and Robert P. Kennedy, eds. *A Reader's Companion to Augustine's Confessions*. Louisville and London: Westminster John Knox, 2003.

Patrides, C. A., and Joseph Wittreich, eds. *The Apocalypse in English Renaissance Thought and Literature*. Ithaca, NY: Cornell University Press, 1984.

Rackin, Phyllis. "On Edgar: Delusion as Resolution." In *Twentieth Century Interpretations of King Lear: A Collection of Critical Essays*. Edited by Janet Adelman. Englewood Cliffs, NJ: Prentice-Hall, 1978. Pp. 123–5.

Rice, Julian C. "The Empathic Edgar: Creativity as Redemption in *King Lear*." *Studia Mystica* 7 (1984) 50–60.

Schwehn, Mark. "*King Lear* beyond Reason." *First Things* 36 (1993) 25–33. Online at https://www.firstthings.com/article/1993/10/king-lear-beyond-reason-love-and-justice-in-the-family.

Szabo, I. B. "Robed Man of Justice: The Hermeneutics of Testimony and *King Lear*." *Journal of Literature and Theology* 3 (1989) 331–40.

Vaught, Carl G. *The Journey toward God in Augustine's Confessions. Books I – VI*. Albany: State University of New York Press, 2003.

Warren, M. J. "Quarto and Folio *King Lear* and the Interpretation of Albany and Edgar." In *William Shakespeare's King Lear*. Edited by Harold Bloom. New York: Chelsea House, 1987. Pp. 45–56.

Wetzel, James. "Book Four: The Trappings of Woe and Confession of Grief." In *A Reader's Companion to Augustine's Confessions*. Edited by Kim Paffenroth and Robert P. Kennedy. Louisville, TN, and London: Westminster John Knox, 2003. Pp. 53–69.

Williams, G. W. "Petitionary Prayer in *King Lear*." *South Atlantic Quarterly* 85 (1986) 360–73.

Williams, Rowan. *The Tragic Imagination*. The Literary Agenda. Oxford: Oxford University Press, 2016.

Wittreich, Joseph. "*Image of That Horror": History, Prophecy, and Apocalypse in King Lear*. San Marino, CA: Huntington Library, 1984.

Wittreich, Joseph. "'Image of That Horror': The Apocalypse in *King Lear*." In *The Apocalypse in English Renaissance Thought and Literature*. Edited by C. A. Patrides and Joseph Wittreich. Ithaca, NY: Cornell University Press, 1984. Pp. 175–206.

Wills, Garry. *Saint Augustine's Conversion*. New York: Penguin, 2004.

INDEX